My Argument With The Gestapo
A MACARONIC JOURNAL

I sacrifice this Iland unto thee,
And all whom I lov'd there, and who lov'd mee;
When I have put our seas 'twixt them and mee
Put thou thy sea betwixt my sinnes and thee.

Donne

By Thomas Merton

THE ASIAN JOURNAL
COLLECTED POEMS
EIGHTEEN POEMS
GANDHI ON NON-VIOLENCE
THE GEOGRAPHY OF LOGRAIRE
THE LITERARY ESSAYS
MY ARGUMENT WITH THE GESTAPO
NEW SEEDS OF CONTEMPLATION
RAIDS ON THE UNSPEAKABLE
SEEDS OF CONTEMPLATION
SELECTED POEMS
THE WAY OF CHUANG TZU
THE WISDOM OF THE DESERT
THOMAS MERTON IN ALASKA
ZEN AND THE BIRDS OF APPETITE

About Thomas Merton

WORDS AND SILENCE: ON THE POETRY OF THOMAS MERTON
by Sister Thérèse Lentfoehr

Published by
New Directions

THOMAS MERTON
My Argument
With The Gestapo

A MACARONIC JOURNAL

A NEW DIRECTIONS BOOK

Ex parte ordinis
Imprimi potest:
> Fr. Vincentius Hermans
> Procurator General, Rome
> 10 October 1968

Manufactured in the United States of America
Originally published clothbound in 1969 by Doubleday & Company, Inc.
First published as New Directions Paperbook 403
(ISBN: 0–8112–0586–x) in 1975
Published simultaneously in Canada by Penguin Books Canada Limited

New Directions Books are published for James Laughlin
by New Directions Publishing Corporation,
80 Eighth Avenue, New York 10011

FIFTH PRINTING

AUTHOR'S PREFACE

One Sunday morning in the spring of 1932 I was hiking through the Rhine Valley. With a pack on my back I was wandering down a quiet country road among flowering apple orchards, near Koblenz. Suddenly a car appeared and came down the road very fast. It was jammed with people. Almost before I had taken full notice of it, I realized it was coming straight at me and instinctively jumped into the ditch. The car passed in a cloud of leaflets and from the ditch I glimpsed its occupants, six or seven youths screaming and shaking their fists. They were Nazis, and it was election day. I was being invited to vote for Hitler, who was not yet in power. These were future officers in the SS. They vanished quickly. The road was once again perfectly silent and peaceful. But it was not the same road as before. It was now a road on which seven men had expressed their readiness to destroy me.

That was about the closest I ever really came to direct contact with Nazi violence in its overt form. What this novel is about is really something different. It is about the crisis of civilization in general, and the Germany it deals with is still largely that of Bismarck and the Kaiser. It is the

Germany that *accepted* Nazism. Nazism itself was beyond me!

The book was written in the summer of 1941, when I was teaching English at St. Bonaventure University. I wanted to enter the Trappists but had not yet managed to make up my mind about doing so. This novel is a kind of sardonic meditation on the world in which I then found myself: an attempt to define its predicament and my own place in it. That definition was necessarily personal. I do not claim to have gained full access to the whole myth of Europe and the West, only to my own myth. But as a child of two wars, my myth had to include that of Europe and of its falling apart: not to mention America with its own built-in absurdities.

Obviously this fantasy cannot be considered an adequate statement about Nazism and the war. The death camps were not yet in operation. America was not yet involved. The things that were to come could, at best, be guessed at: but even the wildest and most apocalyptic guesses would never have imagined the inhumanities that soon became not only possible but real. In the face of such things, this book could never have been written so lightly. Therefore the reader must remember that it was dreamed in 1941, and that its tone of divertissement marks it as a document of a past era.

What remains actual about it of course is this: the awareness that, though one may or may not escape from the Nazis, there is no evading the universal human crisis of which they were but one partial symptom.

Abbey of Gethsemani—January 1968

A NOTE ON THE AUTHOR AND THIS BOOK

On December 10, 1968, Thomas Merton died at the age of fifty-three in Bangkok, Thailand, where he had gone to attend a meeting of Abbots of all the Catholic Monastic Orders in Asia. He was born on January 31, 1915, in Prades, France, the older of two boys. His parents were both artists, his father a New Zealander and his mother an American. In 1916 the family moved to the United States, and when Mrs. Merton died five years later, the two boys lived with her parents for some years. In 1925 Merton returned to France with his father and attended the Lycée Ingres at Montauban. When he was fourteen they went to live in England and Merton entered Oakham School, in Rutland. Two years later (1931) his father died in London from a brain tumor. It was his wish that his son should complete his education in England, so Merton remained at Oakham, spending his vacations with family friends or traveling in Europe. In 1933 he won a scholarship to Clare College, Cambridge, but after one year he returned to his maternal grandparents' home in Douglaston, Long Island, and entered Columbia University in 1935, receiving his B.A. in 1938 and his M.A. in 1939.

On December 10, 1941, he entered the Order of Cistercians of the Strict Observance (Trappists), a silent, contemplative order, at Gethsemane, Kentucky. He expected to give up entirely his early ambition to be a writer, but after some years of rigorous training in the Trappist life and studying for the priesthood (he was ordained in 1949) he was encouraged by his abbot to write again. His first published book was *Thirty Poems* (New Directions, 1944). In 1948 his first prose work, *The Seven Storey Mountain,* was brought out and became an almost immediate international best-seller. It was followed by some thirty or more books of prose, poetry, and translation. For many years Merton was considered to be one of the leading writers in the world on the spiritual life, but recently he had more and more turned his attention to matters that had always deeply concerned him—peace, civil rights, ecumenism—and to a subject that had interested him since his undergraduate days, the religions of the Far East.

In thinking of Thomas Merton as a monk (since 1965 a hermit living alone in the woods near the abbey) it is sometimes hard for people to understand his passionate interest in the problems of our time. The fact is the monks are no longer so sheltered from the world that they do not know what is happening outside their own walls, and Merton carried on a vast correspondence, read prolifically, and received visitors from all over the world and from all walks of life. It was not really possible for him to shut out the world. Even in the peaceful wooded hills of Kentucky he could hear the distant boom of the guns at Fort Knox and write: "I have seen the SAC plane, with the bomb in it, fly low over me and I have looked up out of the woods directly at the closed bay of the metal bird with a scientific egg in its breast!" More and more, it seems to me, the concerns of the last years of his life were the same concerns that occupied him in 1940, when I first made the acquaintance of a blond young man who had a novel he wanted published.

I had just come from England and was working in the

book department of Curtis Brown, Ltd., a literary agency. Tom actually brought me two novels, *The Labyrinth* and *The Man in the Sycamore Tree.* I wanted very much to sell them, but while young editors all seemed to share my enthusiasm, older and wiser (and perhaps later sadder?) heads always seemed to prevail. *The Labyrinth* was autobiographical, and Tom said of it in *The Seven Storey Mountain:* "I found the writing of it easier and more amusing if I mixed up a lot of imaginary characters in my own story. It is a pleasant way to write. When the truth got dull, I could create a diversion with a silly man called Terence Metrotone. I later changed him to Terence Park, after I showed the first draft of the book to my uncle, who abashed me by concluding that Terence Metrotone was a kind of acrostic for myself. That was, as a matter of fact, very humiliating, because I had made such a fool of the character."

It is my recollection that *The Man in the Sycamore Tree,* which was a wild and wonderful story, often extremely funny, also had in it a strong autobiographical streak. Unfortunately it was presumably one of the three finished novels that he himself destroyed before entering the Abbey of Gethsemane.

The third book that Tom brought to the literary agency was *Journal of My Escape from the Nazis,* now called *My Argument with the Gestapo.* I liked it and again tried to sell it, but this was even tougher. It was 1941. How could one interest anyone in a book about an *imaginary* visit to England and France. Newsmen, broadcasters, well-known authors, statesmen were all experiencing the Blitz and the Occupation of France firsthand and writing copiously about it. To complicate matters, Tom's attitude toward the picture of brave little England and his sharp remarks on such sacred subjects as allied propaganda were considered at best puzzling, at worst downright suspicious. There was the difficulty of the macaronic passages with their jumble of

English, French, Spanish, German, Italian, and who knows
what else. And the double-talk—surely a sign of the impact
of Finnegans Wake on our whole generation—did not tend
to help things at all.

I do not recall that the book was offered extensively to
publishers. There seemed no use in trying to buck contem-
porary public opinion, however much I admired the book
personally. In any case, shortly thereafter Merton went off
to enter a Trappist monastery, news that infuriated me, as
I imagined that this author of so much promise was now lost
forever behind a high stone wall of silence. It seemed particularly sad because he had so passionately wanted to be
published and had never appeared to doubt for one minute
that he was destined to be a successful author.

As the world knows now, his faith in his gift was well
founded, and my lamentations proved unwarranted. Some
seven or eight years later Tom came back into my life with
the manuscript of *The Seven Storey Mountain*. From time to
time during the years between 1949 and 1967, when we were
corresponding regularly about his work and meeting at the
abbey occasionally, he raised the question of publishing *My
Argument with the Gestapo,* as it is now called. Of all his
early books this was the one he had never been able to
abandon. I think the reason is clear. The book expresses his
lifelong convictions about the futility of war and its brutal-
izing effects on man. Far from changing his youthful ideals
he had come full circle and now felt more than ever obliged
to speak out against the immorality and callousness of nu-
clear warfare, to urge, whenever and wherever he could
make himself heard, the urgent necessity of world peace, of
a true understanding of the inherent dignity of man, all
men, everywhere.

He wrote me in September 1967: "The next book I hope
to deliver will be, unless you strongly object, the JOURNAL
OF MY ESCAPE [*My Argument with the Gestapo*]. I have

gone over it making a few minor changes, and it is now being typed. I do think it reads well, just as well as it ever did (at least to me) and I think this is a reasonable time to try it out again. I hope you agree."

I admit to having some qualms. Early works are often better left in the attic, and we had both been a lot younger in 1941. As I reread the book, I was delighted with it. I had forgotten how many scenes from his boyhood were in it, and doubt if I had even noticed originally the signs of his growing interest in the monastic life.

It was a great happiness to Tom to know that at last it would really happen; the book would be issued in the summer of 1969, virtually as it was written twenty-eight years ago.

Naomi Burton

St. Valentine's Day, 1969
York, Maine

I

JOURNAL: LONDON

I am carried away by the same wind that blows all these people down the street, like pieces of paper and dead leaves, in all directions.

The sky has faded, between the roofs of buildings where men in helmets stand, pointing upward. Very high, shining like flying papers, sliding out of the updraft of big buildings into the darkening clouds, I see the two very small and distant bombers.

Window glass falls all around me like a shower of money. In my dream I see the slow-motion breaking of the building half a mile away. The explosion hits me in the chest like a football, and I spring backwards over the somersaulting sidewalks.

I have only been here a few hours. I don't know where to go, what kind of a sign to look for, where I will see the arrows that point to doors in the earth. Up, high, between the buildings, I see the small flashing bombers blowing about, sideways and backwards, in the sky; through all the opening windows of the buildings, noise flies out like bees. I begin to run.

Men fly past me in the other direction, unrolling a hose

as they go. I remember in my dream the place where I used to go to buy Duke Ellington records ("Jungle Nights in Harlem," "Wall Street Wail," "Cotton Club Stomp") because it was in a cellar. You entered a triangular shop on a corner, walked among pianos, to the stairs. Down below were booths and silent carpets and ashtrays. I look into all the doorways, running through the street that begins to smell of smoke.

A man on the corner waves me back as I run toward him: a man in a black suit and a helmet. He is outlined against the clouds of yellow smoke that look, in my dream, like gas. He lifts his arms at me, he points back the way I have come.

"Go back!" he cries. "Get into the Underground! Green Park Station is behind you!"

The walls of all the buildings roar down at me like waterfalls. Five men run down off the top of a stopped bus. The last one has his arm full of bundles.

Hurriedly, in the entrance to the Underground, the man ahead of me buys copies of all the different papers, then the paper seller gets all his papers together and follows the customer to the escalator, with me behind them both.

The tunnel where the escalator goes down roars like a barrel full of sea wind. My head is full of thunder. I am carried downward into the earth. In my hand is a long white ticket marked one penny.

I begin to prepare myself for the sad and gallant smiles of the people sitting along the platforms, down below, like souls waiting for the boatman Charon, by the black river of hell.

I prepare to face the solemn little children, crowded together in the bottom of this pit, wearing the wise, sharp, tired-out faces of old men.

The sound of the lamentable, croaking, gay songs they have been singing, down there, to the tune of the broken accordions, makes me shudder in my sleep.

Already I hear the patter of the jugglers, and see the rotten teeth in the smiles of the starving tenors that entertained, of old, the Pit Queues outside Wyndham's Theatre or the Hippodrome. Already I see the caps of the organ grinders and the camp stools of the patient old women waiting for the doors to let them in: and already I hear the sick joy in the voice of the singer, his tired gaiety, and his weak and despairing innuendos; already I feel the full terror of the sickbed gaiety of the bombed music halls, the gaiety that has been playing since Christmas to these frightened people in the tubes.

But at midnight, the accordion players will stop their terrible songs, and the last train will pass out of the station. Then, thousands of people will plunge down from the platform into the pit of the tracks, and lie down, wrapped in coats and rugs and newspapers between the steel rails, and rest their heads on the ties.

The dim lights will shine in silence on the concrete vault.

In the midst of the quietness, I remain awake, listening for the faint rumor of breathing to rush along the sides of the tunnel. A sleeper suddenly cries out: the cry flies out of the tunnel and echoes on the shining tiles.

A witty ghost sits up and swears painfully. The whole vault begins to ring with tubercular coughing.

I feel the shaking of the earth above me, or else imagine it, for I know how the bombs break down the dirty labyrinth, bursting big houses like erupting volcanoes, and scattering bricks like confetti.

On every step of the unmoving escalator a body lies, wrapped in some drab garment, laid in a broken, angular shape. I cannot get out of the sick, sour smell of the subway full of people.

Noise is heard from the city above us. Once more some

sleepers sit, awake, with eyes wide open as if they had never slept at all.

An old man comes up to me:

"What nationality are you?" he says. "You are not English. Where do you come from, to see us English people in our silent, incomprehensible courage? What do the people in your country think of our resistance? Do they know how brave we are? Do they understand our bravery?"

"Nobody understands your bravery," I answer him, "and least of all, I."

"You don't talk like an Englishman," he answers, "and yet you do, too. A foreigner, educated in England, are you? What is your country? Surely you come from some democracy."

"It would be hard to say what country I belong to."

All the people, now, are sitting up, holding their wrappings around them, looking about and listening to the increasing sound of the raid that renews itself above us in the city. Some stand up.

Somebody shouts out, "They have hit Buckingham Palace!" as if there were any way of knowing what had been hit: but another voice answers, like a challenge:

"Maybe they have, but the King and Queen are safe."

That is what was wanted: the sound of a cheer, wild and mournful, begins to spread all through the crowd. Near me, I hear an old woman crying out:

"The King and Queen don't have to hide in the Underground. Only we poor come down under the earth: we are the most afraid, yet the most loyal."

Another woman cries, with the shiver of hysteria in her shrill yell:

"If any persons are above, there, trying to get through the gates, to get in the Underground now, they are too late. They are too late, I tell you. There is no room for any more persons down here, and no more will be allowed. If you are trying to get down here now, you are out of luck!"

"No more will be allowed," cries a man. Around him, in a confused babble, a scribble of mouths makes the response: "hear hear! hear hear! hear hear!" (like a party in Parliament).

But then the whole earth shakes with a giant bomb above us, so great that spontaneously, all over the tunnel, voices begin at once the words of the very same song, together: a song full of lying gaiety, cloaked in smut.

"Listen to them," says the man who has been talking to me. "You say you do not know your own nationality. Then if you have no national pride, how can you expect to understand our bravery?"

"I have lived in too many countries to have a nationality," I answer, "but I like to be free."

"Listen to them singing" (and the stupid, dirty drinking song spreads through the whole crowd). "Listen to our cockney pluck, our limey smut!"

(They are said to have sung hymns on the sinking *Titanic*. I do not say they should sing at all.)

I see a man as thin as sticks and skin, standing up and leading the song, wagging his toothless mouth, waving his cap. He has a Woodbine cigarette stuck behind his ear.

"You will never understand our pluck," says my interlocutor.

"Perhaps not."

"It is what we are fighting for," says the old man, "that makes us plucky."

All at once the singing has died out, as spontaneously as it began. Without either demonstration or applause, the song ends. They all got sick of it, at the same time. They sit down again, bravely, and some of them turn over to go to sleep.

"Do you think you know what freedom is?" says the man.

"Yes, I know what it means to me."

"But probably not what it means to us."

"Why are you fighting?" I ask him. "Tell me clearly, what for: not in the language of politicians. Tell me some concrete things you are fighting for."

"We are fighting for Cadbury's chocolate, for Woodbines, for the London County Council, for the Gasworks, for the Doulton Pottery at Lambeth, and for the broken span in the middle of the Waterloo Bridge. We are fighting for Lord Nelson's blind eye, his last words ("Kiss me, Hardy"), and his notorious mistress, Lady Hamilton, as portrayed in our films by Vivien Leigh. We are fighting not only for the spot where the Crystal Palace used to stand, but also for the Surrey Oval. We are, above all, fighting for the time Seaman Watson beat Walter Neusel in the Albert Hall: that's England over Germany, every time. We're bound to win."

"The whole world," I say, "is appalled at the courage of that wizened kid over there, sitting up like an old man, unable to sleep, unable to speak, unable to cry."

"But the Americans," says the man, "they understand us: they are just like us. They understand that happy nipper, sheltered in our plucky Underground. And what about you? Don't your people understand us at all?"

I shake my head and ask him:

"What will happen when the air raids stop? Will the big black Kaffir dressed in feathers, who sold me a bad tip at Windsor in the autumn of '32, appear once more at Alexandra Park? Will you rebuild the bricks of Bermondsey in England's green and pleasant land, and cry through London's chartered streets the victories of Tottenham Hotspur, the defeats of Brentford?"

"You don't understand us," he says. "We are fighting just for the pluck."

"But there'll always be an Oxo, always be a Bovril?"

"Why not?" says the old man. "We're brave enough to deserve them!"

And when I next look up the escalator, up which there is no escape over the broken, bended bodies, I begin to think: "What if I now saw blue smoke make tendrils down the long escalator toward us? What if they sent down gas? What if, while we were here, the Government had agreed with the Germans, and all had turned against the poor, hiding in their shelters in confusion, and sent down, into their hiding places, in all the warring countries, the gas?

I cannot sleep, for the infinite confusion of sounds where hundreds of people are coughing out their lungs, in these dim tunnels.

II

JOURNAL: LONDON

The wind harps of the all-clear signal ring in the four gray corners of the sky, which is beginning to empty of smoke. It is dawn. The people are coming out of the ground.

I stand in the street, while, away from me, they disperse in every direction. The bus that was abandoned outside the tube station last night is now crowded again. It is turning carefully in the street littered with bricks, ready to head back towards the City, from which it did not get far, last night.

The man who had bundles under his arm to take home has them still under his arm, returning to work. The people all hang their heads in shame, as though they were going home from a debauch.

The sirens let their song trail down and die on the damp and smoky air of burning London.

I am left alone in the street, and listen to the whispering fire on top of the Berkeley Hotel. By its nearness and innocence, the fire talks happily to me, and I am comforted by the close, familiar cursing of the firemen, who even now have it under control.

But from behind the clearing smoke, and the sounds immediately near, comes the more terrifying, more mysterious sound, the sound of the nightmare-talking of all London, half distinguishable: the terrible simultaneous choirs of distant slums lamenting in the dawn.

For now I hear the tears of Camden Town, wounded, somewhere beyond the faces of these complacent buildings, and I hear the far-off mourning cries of Islington, Aldgate, Whitechapel, Mile End. Due east, through the city's greatest thickness, come to me the crowded voices of Limehouse and Stepney, Tower Hill and Bermondsey, and Wapping, and the Isle of Dogs.

Deeper and clearer, to my left, Kentish Town and Marylebone lament. Farther off and more confused, to my right, the city's south, Lambeth and Battersea. Behind me, towns I saw through the windows of the District Railway in my childhood: Hammersmith, Acton, Putney, Shepherd's Bush.

Then it begins to rain, and when the first drops fall heavily and audibly upon the street, I hear also a fireman, on the roof of the Berkeley, utter a sharp, harsh cry of tired laughter, and he waves his arms in relief.

I have nowhere to go, but I walk eastward, against the direction of the softly blowing smoke, walking only to beguile my weariness.

I pay no attention to a woman, an air raid warden, in a helmet, who comes out of a ruined shop, holding in her hand a flashlight. But when I am already past her, her soft, hoarse voice speaks my name, and I turn around.

"You," she says, "Merton!"

I do not know her. I have never seen the face in the shadows of that helmet.

"What are you doing here?" she says.

I hesitate and say, "Who is it?"

She takes the helmet off, her face comes out of the shadow, her brown hair falls heavily about her neck. In the midst of her smoky skin, I see her eyes, and recognize her.

"It is you, B.!"

"What are you doing in England? Have you been back here all this time, since the war started?"

"No, I have only been back a day."

"Why do you come back now?"

"Not to fight."

"Where have you been?"

"Everywhere. And you: married?"

"No. Have you got a cigarette?"

"I don't smoke any more."

She calls out, "Hey," to a man standing with his coat collar turned up, under the entrance to Burlington Arcade, out of the rain, and she catches the package of Players' he throws her.

We sit down together in the ruined shop. A couple of hats lie crumpled in the broken glass upon the floor. Hatboxes are blown into the far corner, off the shelves, in a cluttered heap. The shelves, having collapsed, slant along the wall, askew. She says:

"Why do you come back now?"

"To see what it is like in the Green Park tube station on a night like last night."

"Is that all?"

"No. I also came back to see how much last night would be like the other nights I remember in London. I have come to make sure the sleeplessness of the air raids is the same as the sleeplessness of the nightmares in the shuttered rooms of the past years."

"Will you write about it?"

"How did you know?"

"What will you say?"

"I will say that it is true: the things I remember are destroyed, but that does not mean as much as it seems, because the destruction was already going on before, and destruction is all I remember."

"What are some things you have seen destroyed?"

"Lottie Crump's house, in Evelyn Waugh's *Vile Bodies*, the houses in *Antic Hay*, and the hotel where the orchestra played 'What's He to Hecuba?'"

"No, not that hotel: that was the Berkeley, wasn't it?"

"Perhaps. I am not trying to be accurate, except symbolically."

"What else?" she says. "What else will you have to say?"

"I will say that last night in the tube station I remembered the flat, harsh songs of street singers, the frightful puns of the crippled magicians, and the bravery of blind accordion players. But when the street singing in the tubes came to an end, the sound receded like water in the tunnel, and the full horror of a Seven Dials' doss house filled with the dying poor became the only reality in the world: then I remembered how I once lay on pallets in doss houses, out of bravado, yet went sleepless because of the noise of those who *had* to sleep there, eternally coughing out the heavy, ragged bladders of their lungs.

"And I will say this morning I remembered the thick-walled houses of the doctors and dentists north of Oxford Street, and the stuffy halls of family hotels.

"I will write about the small room I once slept in, one that smelled of fog and quilts, in a temperance place. All night long I could hear water murmuring in the pipes in the wall, and the voices of old ladies came through the frail locked door—thin voices of people roaming quietly on the stairs like wraiths in *The Aeneid*, gathering around a saucer of blood.

"I will bring to mind all the places where I ever tried to sleep, in the old days, in London, when there was supposed to be peace. The nightmares I had then may make comprehensible these raids."

While I talk, B. flicks the cigarette, with her finger, out

the big hole where the plate-glass shop front used to be, and I continue:

"Perhaps the things I remember in nightmares are the things everybody is really fighting for."

B. says quietly, "I cannot understand you any more. You talk in a way I have forgotten how to understand. Understanding no longer means the same thing to both of us. If that is the way you have come here to interpret the war, it would have been better if you had stayed away."

"I am not looking for the easy level on which it seems to be comprehensible and really is not," I reply.

"The level of the fighters?"

"Yes. The opinions of politicians and soldiers have no meaning for me. But there must be other meanings, on another level, and I have come to look for them."

"And looking for them you talk about this war as if it were the war of Troy."

"The war of Troy is completely understandable."

"But this is not the war of Troy, and you are living in the midst of it. I am sad that you came back, with your talk about meanings." So she puts on her helmet again. We both get up. A group of firemen go marching by outside, in disorder, and fire trucks clatter by leaving the riot of echoes among the city's houses, the ruined and the whole.

B. gives me a slip of paper with her phone number.

"Come and see me," she says, "when I am not so tired. Maybe I will have remembered how to talk."

III

JOURNAL: LONDON

In how many strange rooms in London have I awakened
and lain in bed, sometimes loving the pale sun in the
window, sometimes loving the smell of tea on the stairs,
sometimes loving the sound of water running into a bath,
or the sight of Christmas fogs: but how much oftener have
I awakened to hate the blackness of the days, the wet wind
stirring the sooty curtains, the voices of the foreigners on the
stairs, and the sound of water weeping in the confinement
of the air shafts on which my window opens!

The top-floor halls of the Regent Palace are an interminable labyrinth of tunnels, where the embezzler's foot falls
snugly on the carpets, and the room doors barely close upon
the furtive hatred of the thief for his sick woman.

I fear this pale and yellow light, and the sound of so
many dishonest voices in the Regent Palace. The room I
was once supposed to wake up in was right up under the
roof: supposing I had to sleep there now?

I dream of walking in those interminable halls, full of
people. Scared cheats lurk in the doorways wearing old
school ties to which they are not entitled. They are everywhere, talking furtively to hide the miaowing in their

speech, but looking out with eyes full of poison from the shadows of their fear. The wrecks of women and men come and go in and out, wooden and white and dead.

When I was last in those endless and dimly lighted passages, I had already learned to fear the sound of bombers filling the air with copper bees, and making the thin roof tremble like a piece of paper.

Now in the nightmare I see the glass-topped table in my narrow room, I see the huge wardrobe that smells of damp, and I see the whole room, with its bed made to imitate the beds of Statler Hotels in America, and I see cards and advices left lying neatly in places where they will be seen, like the advertising you read when you arrive dog-tired in Buffalo at midnight.

I lock the doors of my dream behind me, and take out of my pocket the letter of introduction that has been given to me to a man in the Foreign Office, who will arrange for me to be transported out of the reach of those who pursue me.

The sealed envelope bears the name of Sir A., whom I will not be able to see. He has left London, secretly, and no one knows when he will return.

(The voices of the cheats and imposters whisper in the hall. Once again I make sure I have turned the key in the door's weak lock. Across the deep black street, the other building sleeps with shrouded, undecipherable windows, like a dope fiend. Below, on the sidewalks, I can watch the geometry of prostitution, working itself out in neat, quiet patterns.)

The letter, lying on the glass desk, is too much for me.

It is no use resisting my curiosity now. I tear the letter open, and read:

"The bearer is under no circumstances to be allowed to leave the Regent Palace Hotel. It is even more important that he never suspect that he has been recognised, and he must therefore be treated with supercilious condescension, but some tact. However he will be locked in his room and kept there until further orders, namely, the orders that will definitely name the date and place of his execution."

I wake myself with the cry of terror leaping in my throat.

There was a rooming house in Bloomsbury where an Indian Ph.D. committed suicide. I remember the smell of clammy washrags on the marble-topped washstand.

Once I woke up in the night and was scared by something I couldn't name, but I leaped out of bed and put on my clothes and ran downstairs and out into the sweet-smelling fog.

It was two in the morning. I had forgotten to bring my key.

It did not matter that the door had slammed behind me. I hurried down the street, remembering only how I had sat up suddenly, leaping out of my sleep, wide awake and with fear bundled up in my stomach like a fist. Even if it hadn't been too late to ring the bell and go back for my key, I wouldn't have gone back anyway.

I ended up in a basement in Soho called a night club.

The walls were hung with tatters of pictures of bodies, torn out of magazines. The room smelled of cold-blooded women with small eyes and metal teeth. You could hear their hard laughter, and see the frightened faces of the men, who were even then cautiously reaching out their silver money across the bare tables.

Misers danced to a victrola on a little square of linoleum, amid the bickering voices of the women who moved about the floor like iron and steel machines.

Two monsters came uninvited and sat down at my table, where I had a bottle of whiskey and a compulsory gray sandwich.

"We'll mike 'im smile, Flo! Won't we just! 'e's so solemn!" says one.

I don't look up.

"Cough, Flo! Get the gentleman's attention! Pretending not to notice two poor lonely girls!"

The waiter brings two glasses.

I say:

"Emportez ces verres! Foutez ces femmes à la porte! Elles me dégoutent, flanquez les dehors!"

"Ow, 'e's foreign."

"Or pretending to be. Are you French, ducky? Come on, be a sport! Invite us to stay!"

They help themselves to drinks from the bottle and raise the glasses, and start to drink.

I take the bottle off the table, and ram the cork into it, and stick it under my coat and walk out.

Then I wander around in the streets, circling among the narrow lanes and side streets, getting closer and closer to Piccadilly. I begin to get tired. I take the bottle from under my coat, and uncork it, but before I raise it to my mouth the idea nauseates me.

I fling the bottle smash against the side of a house, where it leaves a dark splash on the bricks. I walk on around and around among the streets of the West End, half asleep and half drunk.

Some of the houses are locked and hollow and sad with the tears of vices hidden within them; others are white and blissful, enclosed in their own innocence. I think of the old ladies with the absurd ideas of children, and of young sleepers who drag at their flesh in their sleep with their tired nails. Until at last it begins to get light. The women have left the doorways and gone back to the mews behind the houses of the rich. Then I return to the room where the Indian gave himself that poison.

IV

JOURNAL: LONDON

London was once one city for me, and became, at a certain definite time, another. Both cities are being bombed, and both are real, but they cannot both be real to the same person at the same time, and the city that is being bombed is the one I discovered last. It is the real one, the actual city. The other is only in the mind. It no longer exists.

One London is a city of angels, of good, well-mannered children in their flannel suits and school caps, as simple as trees and plants, as quiet as birds in the evening; the children who walk to church two by two with prayer books in their hands, among the quiet houses, the parks full of lawns and flowers; remembering among the white seventeenth-century spires the grass of the country that opens all around them not far behind the clean, bright buildings. For these, the streets are full of happy traffic, red buses, shining cars, and kind men walking with their gloves and their rolled-up umbrellas in the sunlight. It is the city of the Chinese ducks in St. James's Park, of the kind bishop walking on the Horse Guards' parade in his black gaiters, of the wonderful movie *Million Dollar Legs*, with W. C. Fields and Jack Oakie and Mary Brian and Andy Clyde and

Hugh Herbert, about the country called Klopstockia that won the Olympic games with a tactic of miracles. It is the London where one is taken out to the National Gallery and then to tea somewhere near there; the London where one spends a long time in front of the shiny models of the Cunard liners in Cockspur Street; and it is the London where every street leads almost at once, after rows of happy houses in Dulwich, out to the North Downs; and over all this city is a great kind arch of sky in summer, kind fogs in the winter that make the whole place like a room full of bright shops, promising Christmas.

Until, suddenly, sometime, not for everybody, and never for the innocent, the masks fall off the houses, and the streets become liars and the squares become thieves and the buildings become murderers.

Then behind the silences of the city's great restraint are clearly heard the voices of all the great dark areas of the slums, the recriminations of hundreds of slowly dying regions full of low, narrow houses and smoke and tears. And then are heard the gaiety of the doomed and their terrible resignation.

Suddenly the good gentlemen take on pale burned faces, and the kind, straight men who have been in India begin to fall apart like bundles of sticks, suddenly untied.

And all around are heard the whisperings in the doorways and the cynicisms of the mews where the whores live, and the thin, cheating euphemisms of the family hotels, the dark resignation of the prisons and the muffled strangled wit of the law courts, the grave, coy antics of the librarians and the essayists and the old men in the museums.

Then is heard the menace of the bombers in the sky, which resembles the great vast murmur of the city, protesting, in mile after mile of smoke and stone, against the sorrows of Charles Dickens, and the sober fair liberalism of George Eliot, a woman full of principles.

This is the city that perishes in great need, slowly, without crying for revenge on the blood of the engineers or of the philanthropists and the progressive thinkers of all the strict, benevolent schools, men who were humanitarians but had no love, only principles, only reasons.

I did not know the second city as long as I listened with joy to the church bells playing in the daylight, and believed in the downs and the country and the trees, and believed that the city also was like the country, and that all people were like that too, and that the rich and the poor all saw the same things: the things the children believed in.

But the first city vanished when I walked the streets of the second at night, when I learned to listen to the gaiety of the taxi drivers turn to ashes, and hear the walls of houses echoing, from street to street, the harlot's curse, and the dead good humor of the crippled beggars who lie to amuse the rich, and the servile obscenity of the songs they whisper in the corners of the bars, with the toothless humanism of their laughter and the good, staunch equalitarianism of their blasphemies.

The first city was as pure and kind as the music of Purcell: but it no longer existed, except in the mind, the minds of some who believed in it, and believed in things that London had been forced to forget. But the second city, which was suddenly revealed at a definite time in my life, and, perhaps, everybody else's, was as terrible as no music at all, as dark as chaos, as inescapable as Fear.

V

JOURNAL: LONDON JUNE 1941

I go to the address B. has given me as hers. It is a big house in Berkeley Square, full of uniformed women and the smell of ether. I stand and wait on a wide, empty parquet floor for an hour. Nothing to sit on.

From the other room come the smell of cigarette smoke and the shrill, cultured voices of the girl ambulance drivers, with their hair done up under their caps. It is like a pavilion after a hockey game, except there is nothing excited about the shrillness, only sarcasm.

Presently one of the uniformed women comes out, in trousers, but with plenty of lipstick.

"You the man that's waiting for B.?"

"Yes."

"Got any cigarettes?"

"Sorry, no."

"B. is going on duty in a minute. She is just getting up. She won't be able to see you for very long. She told me to tell you not to wait, unless you want to."

"I'll wait."

"Very well. You say you haven't any cigarettes?"

"No, I don't smoke."

"Oh, you don't. Okay."

"Do you all live here?" I say. "Or rather, is this where B. lives?"

"There are some cots upstairs. This is where she sleeps."

Then the telephone rings, over in a corner of the room, on the floor. The woman in uniform goes over and answers it, and while she is talking, B. comes in the room, with her face clean, rested and without makeup, a cigarette in her pale lips, and her brown hair down to her shoulders. But she is carrying her helmet in her hand.

"You stayed," she said. "But I can't talk to you much. I have to go on duty."

She starts picking her hair up, to get the helmet on.

"Well," she goes on, "what have you been doing? Writing? Finding out anything?"

"Where are all the people I used to know? Is there anybody in London?"

"I don't know," she replies. "I suppose so."

The other one puts the phone down on the bare floor again, and walks over to us.

B. introduces me to her, and I think her name is Miss Griffiths, but I do not catch it: just then there is a lot of noise, because a truck has just pulled up outside, and five or six women in uniforms and helmets get out and come up the steps, through the wide open door of the house.

Simultaneously, out of the basement door, below the window near which we are standing, come two men without hats, one of them having his left arm in a sling. Downstairs there must be a first aid station.

B. and I stand aside at the door to let the women come through. Then we come out onto the steps.

"Griffiths thinks you're a spy," said B. casually.

"Everybody does, I suppose."

"You've changed quite a bit. Of course it's seven years or more, isn't it, since you were last in England? It is quite unmistakable now that you are a foreigner. But I told her you were an American."

"You don't have to tell her anything."

"But you are an American, aren't you?"

"No."

"Anyway, you've changed. And I'm sorry we couldn't have more of a talk the other day. Are you having any trouble with the censors?"

"Oh no, of course not. They don't see anything I write."

"What do you mean? Aren't you a newspaperman?"

"Oh no."

"What are you writing?"

"A diary."

"Oh, I'm sorry. That's different. I suppose that's why you have such ideas about the war."

"I haven't any ideas about the war."

"That's what I mean. Do the Americans think the way you do?"

"I couldn't say. Their government doesn't, anyway."

"They probably feel the way we did when it started."

"How was that?"

"Like being sick. Nauseated. We had no ideas. We just knew we were in it, and didn't know what was going to happen. It was a nasty feeling. Well, here's my lorry."

She climbs into the front seat of a truck, and shakes hands from there. The driver is another woman, in uniform. There is a man, an oldish man, riding in the back, with his ARP helmet on very straight and prim. I suppose he once worked in some very respectable accounting job.

B. says:

"I just remembered, if you go up to the dog cemetery, in Hyde Park, you might find Mrs. Frobisher having a funeral."

"Perhaps I'll go."

"Give her my love. Good-by!"

I watch the truck drive away, and then walk slowly northward, along the edge of the square.

Soon I come to a place where I have to skirt a pile of bricks that have poured down, breaking through the iron railings in front of one of the houses. A neat hole has been blown right in the front of the house, and taken most of the three floors out of the inside, leaving part of a staircase, and walls covered with wallpaper, and, on each one of the three floors, one on top of the other, a series of three neat white Adam fireplaces.

VI

Mrs. Frobisher was waiting among the small tombstones
with two young army officers, each with his hands behind
his back and a swagger stick in his fist: but their uniforms
were slightly bedraggled, not as sharp and fresh as in peacetime.

"Toby's the sixth," Mrs. Frobisher was saying.

"He was much too big," said one of the officers.

"I don't like to say it," said the other, "but it would have
been more merciful to have had him gassed before the
raids started. Madame Gongora had her dogs put away. It
would have been more sensible and far less sad."

"I am neither sensible nor merciful in that way," said
Mrs. Frobisher. "I respect life."

"It is very sad here," said the other young officer. "Let
us not stay here among the tombs of the dogs."

They all three turned around and faced me as I was coming up the path.

"Look who's here," said Mrs. Frobisher. "I never expected to see you in London, let alone here. Had you heard
about Toby being killed in the raid?"

"B. told me I might find you here."

She introduced the soldiers as Lieutenant Bird and Lieutenant Quinn. They were not more than twenty-two.

"This is Mr. Merton," she said of me. "He has been away from England, and has just come back."

"In time for the fun," said Lieutenant Bird with a rather pinched expression.

"And how is poor B.?" said Mrs. Frobisher. "She must be terribly tired. You know, I took tickets on a bus in the general strike, but that wasn't at all the same thing as this. You boys don't remember the general strike," she added, over her shoulder, to Lieutenants Bird and Quinn, who said:

"Oh, we remember it a little."

We came down out of the dog cemetery into the street. The light of the sun was trying to get through the trees, the trees whose leaves were seared a little around the edges as if by fierce, unnatural heat. This also Mrs. Frobisher saw, with her quick eye, and she immediately said:

"Oh, the poor trees," and then went on, "Do you suppose it will be very long before we can beat Hitler and get a just peace?"

"It is a question of time," said Lieutenant Bird quickly.

"Of course, of course," said Mrs. Frobisher, "but I wish we could get a just peace by October. It was an awfully grim winter."

"We must not think of the end yet," said Lieutenant Quinn. "It may take twenty years or more."

"I really think you're wrong," said Mrs. Frobisher. "I think it will be over in October. Or at most in two years. Judging by the last war, we are at least halfway through by now. But I say it can't last much longer."

"You know," said Lieutenant Bird, "it is being brought home to us that air power makes a difference."

"We can't talk convincingly just at present," said Lieu-

tenant Quinn, "but when our plane production catches up
to theirs, then we shall have our say."

"Every day that passes," said Lieutenant Bird, "they
get weaker and we get stronger. Don't forget, their plants
are being bombed."

"At Danecape Hall," said Mrs. Frobisher, "we have the
carpenters in."

"Were you bombed?" I said.

"Yes. We had terrible luck last month. A German, in a
Heinkel, got the wind up and jettisoned his bombs over the
house. He put a huge hole in the tennis lawn, and blew out
all the windows. Something hit one of the chimneys, and
some of the furniture was thrown about. Then they set fire
to the trees and burned out the laurels, so that the north
side of the house is exposed. Only the stables didn't suffer.
It was rather hard lines, I thought, seeing that they had
miles of moors to throw away their bombs in."

"And Mr. Frobisher?"

"Everybody is all right, fortunately. He is in charge of
the ARP, of course, and can't come away at all. I came to
see if anything could be done about the town house. Our
tenants left when the big raids began in the autumn. Then
Toby was caught in some falling bricks the other night.
Poor thing. I hate to see the animals suffer too!"

We walked in silence toward Marble Arch, where some
men were repairing the street. Inside the gate was the wide
asphalt area where the soapbox speakers used to make their
speeches. I mentioned this.

"I spent some very unhappy Sunday afternoons here,"
I said, "because someone had told me it was interesting and
important to listen to the soapbox speakers."

"We still have them," said Lieutenant Quinn proudly.

"I always thought it was rather jolly, having the soapbox
speakers," said Lieutenant Bird, "a sort of a free show.
They don't have that in Germany."

"All the soapbox speakers are running things in Germany," said Mrs. Frobisher rather slyly. "You know, I always imagined the Germans were fundamentally wiser than the French. How could they ever have let those charlatans get to the position they now hold?"

"I am beginning to doubt if there is anything fundamentally wise about the French," said Lieutenant Quinn sourly. "I hope the Americans will make better allies than the French did."

"I'm sure the Americans will be very co-operative if it is a question of dollars," said Lieutenant Bird.

Then he suddenly looked at me and became a little red.

"Mr. Merton is Australian, and Canadian, rather than American," said Mrs. Frobisher, "aren't you?"

"I have relatives in New Zealand."

"I don't know where we'd be without the Dominions," said Lieutenant Quinn firmly. "They are showing up very well what with Greece, and Crete, and everything."

"And you," said Mrs. Frobisher, "what brings you to England? I suppose you are going into the Air Force."

"No," I said, "I have only come to see what is happening."

"To see what is *happening?*"

"Yes, and perhaps write about it."

"We haven't thought of this as something one would come to *see,*" said Lieutenant Bird quietly, but Lieutenant Quinn said:

"Oh, I suppose you are a reporter."

"In a way. But I was hoping Mrs. Frobisher might be able to tell me where I could find some of my old acquaintances. You mentioned Madame Gongora: I didn't know you knew her."

"I met her during one of the first big raids," said Mrs. Frobisher, "when I took shelter in the Dorchester. That was the first time I ever slept on the floor, but it was nice there.

We are all getting used to sleeping on the floor once in a while."

"I spent the other night in Green Park Station."

"It is very fortunate for the poor that we have such deep tube stations."

"And Madame Gongora?" I said.

They told me the address.

VII

JOURNAL: LONDON

I was more than surprised to know that the Frobishers had made the acquaintance of Madame Gongora, although she is well known to almost everybody in London, except, precisely, people like the Frobishers, who spend most of their time out of London anyway: out of London, isolated with their complicated fads, and utilitarian disciplines, in the Yorkshire moors.

There, in the north, you came to the head of a valley where, every mile or so, you had passed the ruins of a textile mill. Then out into the moors where now, every day, the tanks maneuver. There the infantry run after the tanks with heather all over their hats. Suddenly the games take a serious turn when some enemy planes come over, on the way to bomb one of the cities. The men lie in the heather, and behind the hill the antiaircraft begins to go off rapid and loud. There, in this strange outlandish setting, still flourish strongly the little scientific eccentricities of the Frobishers, things that had begun to die when old Shaw was young and clever and a vegetarian himself.

Here, on the contrary, in the house of Madame Gongora, things are absolutely different.

Here are baroque chandeliers and a grand piano and paintings by Le Douanier Rousseau and, in the dining room, Matisse, and, upstairs, Picasso, Chagall.

Here in the big, surprising house that used to be sometimes quiet and reflective, sometimes filled with all the glass laughter of Madame Gongora's many acquaintances, are, at any rate, no judgments and no opinions. There are statements, but not lectures.

But now it is a time of war. The house has changed. It is still surprising, but in a less peaceful way.

When the windows were blown out here, Madame Gongora had them boarded up. When the roof burned, all the things from the attic were moved down to the drawing room, with the grand piano and the Rousseaus.

Here, then, are a dressmaker's form, a cello, a Dresden fruit dish standing on the table full of small, discarded metal fixtures like picture hangers and doorknobs; a stack of German sheet music, with the names Bach, Mozart, Weber printed on the light green paper in ornate nineteenth-century letters. On the table lie several volumes of the *Histories* of Tacitus, in Latin, and over them, a black lace mantilla that has been unfolded, held up to be looked at, and then carelessly thrown down. In a corner of the room stand some framed paintings on the floor, turned face to the wall.

On the floor, next to the cello, stands a brown box, about the size of a cigar box, open, full of tubes of oil paint. A couple of tubes of paint lie dry and lost outside the box, on the waxed, uncarpeted floor that shines like the parquets at Versailles or Fontainebleau.

All this to one side of the room.

In the midst, between this confusion and the grand piano, in the semidarkness caused by the boarded, blown-out windows, Madame Gongora in a straight-backed chair with a light, camel's-hair coat flung about her shoulders and a flower in her black hair, sits smoking a Balkan cigarette.

Her bodyguard admits me when I speak to him, not in English.

I pass through the white door.

"Cara Madama! Che estonimen! Sorpresi!"

"Caro Monsur!" she says with merry astonishment, raising the hand that holds the cigarette. "Seas bon-ventu! Delizios de vos vidir! Que vos transapor hasta li Londri tanto peligros?"

"Mioioni monoo politiou oho obrastif arto," I reply succinctly.

It is a delight to see Madame Gongora again. She holds out both hands to me, the coat falls off her shoulders, and she is the first woman I have seen in London wearing a real dress, not a uniform or something in serge or tweed. (Mrs. Frobisher, as it happened, was in tweeds at her wolfhound's funeral.)

"Trovesi che sentar, poco confortu, qui: ke mi perdoni, cher! Alli chaise. Sofa ne plus, por cause de lis malfortunant bombardimenti, nocta di Maji 10, cuando lu put out li Bigaben por fragiment bombardieri, como an eye by a fingor, introdusci digito nel oculasti Casa Parlamentesco, si direbbe!"

"Drole. No ho vidit, todavia, lis ruins Casa di Parlamenti. Pocu interes, d'ailleurs. Casa comuni's: Casa Lordo: next time ils bombardir rosbif of old Ingleterro, mi reaccion to mi is to shrug. So quoi!"

"Helas," she agrees, a slight cloud of sadness passing through the dark brightness of her eyes, "edificios mi impresionu poco, cuando bombardit. C'est lous puebolos, uominis y felelas y soppra tutto infantilis, eso si! Che M'astrinsse il cor, stark, tensitif! Merced! No puedo soportar, tal fois." And then she goes on, "Mais usted: ya oublisco di memorar what you disais una minuta pasatz.

Por quoi has usteds venido ici to la Londra? Operas di mision delicado? No, disitz. Y que? Otra chos?"

"Escribcio," I answer simply, "leteratura: arto: poema: jorneli diaristik sobre La Krieg, if you get me, madama."

"Oh yes, writing a book. Caro! Che splendor! Escribcio!"

"Autobiografo, un pocu."

"And a good book too, I hope," she said.

"Claro che si!"

"Nullo comercial. Nullo economist. Mucho nullo politicu? Hey, artisto?"

"Corecto, emfatik nullo politicu!"

"Y escript quoi che placer tu mismo, hey, garzoni? Escript dialectico personal, sin umbrages di folor realist? Escript su proprio esperantu. Bono. Bono. Je vous aime, artisto!"

"Provencau!" I exclaimed with a laugh. "Y doble-parlar."

"Eso fazera exclamar di colera moltos estupidos, che se considreen plurimo robato como di ladron por li vendedor di libro galant, fantastico doble-speech, che no le imparto nullo informacio sur la cultivacio di poultry, chicken's feed, cuisine, basket weaving, how to add sums, how to oil your ersatz auto, how to make shoes, fabrica gross cigars, li comercio di articulos selects, or else tracts about conduct in the tramway, besala mano to Madama some slut, how to make a good matrimonio. Y los ceteros como cosi!"

"Mi Fousto non malo di esos!" I reply with a laugh. "I'll write the way I feel like."

"Bono! Bravo Mertoni! Seas beni-venuto into my pobre casa casi demolits por lis bombardieris tudesks."

VIII

I brought my typewriter and suitcase to Madame Gongora's last night. I am on the second floor, I can see down the street toward the park: I can see the trees. Next to me, as I write, I hear the incessant ticking of a big, cheap alarm clock of American make. There is pale sunlight coming through the window, empty of all glass.

From the outside, this just looks like a bombed house: with the ground-floor windows boarded up and a hole in the roof Actually it is one of the busiest places in London.

I have this whole floor to myself: downstairs lives Madame Gongora: upstairs lives her servant and bodyguard, Valdes. But downstairs there are always people coming and going: all kinds of people.

I translate one of the things she said to me yesterday (this was in answer to one of my questions).

"I cannot tell you where to find all that you are looking for. I cannot tell you where to go to find anything. Everything is so disorganized that if you go around the bombed city looking for a thing or a person or for any information or for any idea, you will not find anything, you will only go out of your mind. The only thing to do is to wait until something comes to you, some news, some money, some preferment. All news sooner or later comes to my house. Why not, then, stay here? Stay here and wait. If the house is not bombed first, the news will probably come walking through the door."

From my window, I can look down on to the front door-step, leading down into this street, which used to be a quiet and clean Mayfair Street. At the moment, it is quiet: but although there are no wounds visible, no ruined houses just within my line of vision, and although all the glass and bricks have been cleared away, this is not a peacetime street: the street is not well.

There is no fresh paint, the houses are tired. The street itself is almost always empty. And although it is not used, it seems to be just about to want repairs: yet at no place can you find the hole that needs to be repaired. Sometimes, men and women come walking along the sidewalks. Just now, three or four women, in olive green uniforms, went riding by silently on bicycles.

From time to time, from the end of the street, comes the deep thunder of a line of army lorries, and the walls of the house shake until they have all gone by.

But all the houses have the expression of patients in a hospital, tired, wondering about themselves, and fearing to be roused from the uneasiness of their secret obsession with disease, by some new; objective alarm, some fresh pain.

Most of the people who come along the street stop under my window. I hear the heavy steps of the bodyguard, Valdes, going along the downstairs hall. Most of the time I cannot hear the words that are spoken, below me, at the door, but sometimes I can recognize the language in which they are said.

So far, today, most of the visitors have been English, all right. But I heard the Hungarian language, and there were two who spoke Spanish, also.

Someday, to this door, will come some person with the news I am waiting for, although I do not know what kind of news it is that I am waiting for. It will not be a definite message, necessarily, and the person may just bring the news unconsciously, carrying it along like a germ with some other words more important to him, bringing the news that is my life or my death, yet no more conscious of it than those bees that fecundate plants by carrying pollen from one to the other, even less respectful of the pollen they carry than a person would be of some dust on his coat.

I don't know what kind of person to look for, and I don't know what language I will hear spoken at the door. Meanwhile, I sit in this room, looking out at the silent, empty-seeming houses. And the houses remain recollected, in the midst of their fear, the fear which they cannot understand.

Suddenly, across the street, on the opposite pavement, stand two men pointing at my window. They are men in dark suits and helmets. The suits are blue serge, and well pressed, too. They have seen me, sitting not far from the window, typewriting. They do not like me, sitting in one of the bombed houses of London, writing on my typewriter.

Now they see me looking at them and writing on my typewriter. They both fold their arms and frown at me from under their helmets.

I stare back at them.

They speak to one another, over there. I see their heads nodding.

Then one of them raises his head, and his voice comes to me easily across the quiet street, without any necessity for shouting:

"You in the window," it says, "is your house empty, or occupied? And if it is empty, what are you doing, typewriting in an empty house?"

"It is occupied," I say. "Can't you see I am in it?"

"It is our business to know which houses are occupied. This is the house of Madame Gongora: has she left it, or is she still living there?"

"She is still here."

"Are you her secretary?"

"I am a writer. I write what I see out of the window. I am writing about the fear on the faces of the houses. I say as fast as I can, what preoccupation I see in the sick houses of bombarded London, and I write that the houses of bombarded London do not understand their own fear."

My words fall into the street with absolutely no echo at all, as clear as if I were talking to myself, and, just as clear and distinct to my ear come the quietly spoken words of the man in the helmet.

"What have you just written about us? Have you written about our courage?"

"I have written that you folded your arms and frowned at me from under the shadows of your helmets. I have not written about your courage."

Now they whisper to one another, again, their heads nod until they turn again to where I am. The other one says (the one who had not spoken before):

"Who are you working for? Why do you write that our houses do not understand their fear: rather write that they do not understand their courage."

"It is the same thing."

"Then what do you know about our courage and our fear? Where do you come from? What is the basis of your statements about us? You say you write what you see, but no two men see the same street, here. What do you see that you write? What do you mean when you talk about our courage and our fear?"

"I am still trying to find out: and that is why I write."

"How will you find out by writing?"

"I will keep putting things down until they become clear."

"And if they do not become clear?"

"I will have a hundred books, full of symbols, full of everything I ever knew or ever saw or ever thought."

"If it never becomes clear, perhaps you will have more books than if it were all clear at once."

"No doubt. But I say if it were all clear at once, I would not really understand it, either. Some things are too clear to be understood, and what you think is your understanding of them is only a kind of charm, a kind of incantation in your mind concerning that thing. This is not understanding: it is something you remember. So much for definitions! We always have to go back and start from the beginning and make over all the definitions for ourselves again."

Now the two men confer together once more, with nodding helmets, and the first one speaks after a minute:

"Say this for our courage. Our courage is like the careless, quiet, grave wit of Ralph Richardson in the films. Say that our bravery is like the humorous valiance of this calm and funny actor, who makes absolutely no judgments about anything, denounces no one, hates no one, is oblivious to the fantastic wars of the films he is in, and, as if by mistake, catches the spy, wins. Say our courage is like this fine preposterous actor's, say it is humorous, and ignores all the bad rhetoric, and ignores the war itself. Our courage parodies the war, and burlesques the serious war, refuses to understand wars, and wins them by luck. Say our courage is this: that we believe we are above the war by our humor and our instinctive nicety of feeling, and that if we cling to what we know is humorous and sincere, if we make no wrong gestures, we will, in the end, catch the spy, as if by mistake, and it will be over. Then we can walk off gravely and humorously with our hat over our eye."

"You speak for the whole of England?" I ask him.

"In a way. The whole of England does not know this,

but aspires to it, because it is the one thing left in England to aspire to: the goodness of these gentle, subtle, and jolly detectives who catch the spy, as if by mistake."

"If that is true, your courage is a kind of perfection. You cannot understand your fear because it attacks you subtly like an animal sickness, and is not capable of being understood, is only suffered, and then goes away again, at once, after a trial of your exemplary patience. The fear is not the fear of being hurt or captured or killed by the enemy, but of becoming like the enemy himself: becoming a person who believes in war. Your courage is to believe you can win a war without believing in the war itself, that you can catch the spy by laughing at your own mistakes, and that the spy is caught chiefly because he cannot laugh at himself?"

"Our courage," said the stranger, "always evades the cruelty and cleverness of the enemy because of its own spontaneous wit, not because of any plan or any greater cleverness: we win only by laughter. Our courage is like Robert Donat, pursued by grim Scotch detectives on one side and terrible German spies posing as Scotch detectives on the other, wanted by the English for a supposed murder and by the Germans because he knows their secret. And he escapes from them both into a hall full of people waiting for a political speech, blunders on to the stage, in his haste, is applauded, announced as the speaker.

"Then, standing in the middle of the stage, and beginning to see, already, the Germans sidle into the back of the hall through one door, and the detectives through another, he makes a short, funny, parody political speech which puts the whole audience into a great, enthusiastic good humor, until they laugh and shout and applaud him wildly. And in the midst of the applause he is led out handcuffed by the Germans, posing as detectives, and the applause follows him out of the hall, and he is taken away in a car, until, soon, he makes another escape. That is how our courage is. It is not animal courage, but a wonderful, subtle, and happy versatility that evades all the animal serious-ness of those who believe in wars, and we shall conquer because we shall be lucky. We are so humorous our luck can never fail."

"You say you speak for the whole of England? I do not believe you."

"I can say that because that is what we most love to see in the films: this lucky detective."

Then I leaned on the window sill and looked at these two well-dressed strangers in their helmets and I said:

"I do not believe what you say applies to anybody but yourselves. The courage you dream of is a kind of humorous perfection, but the courage of the English has to be under-stood differently, if it can be understood at all."

"Then do you know what our courage consists in?"

"No."

"What does it mean to you, then?"

"Very little. I cannot understand why the men that came in black hundreds out of the hotels and onto the dunes of Dunkerque and staggered into the sea where rowboats were waiting to take them in twos and threes to England, I can-not understand why these men did not go mad with the songs that ran over and over in the same broken grooves of their minds, during that escape.

"I do not understand those soldiers, blind with weariness and confusion and weakness, wading away from the fires among the dunes, with nothing in their heads but: 'Oh Johnny, Oh Johnny, how you can love. Oh Johnny, Oh Johnny, Oh Johnny,' until the low-flying Messerschmitts got them with their machine guns.

"I do not understand the thousand sailors of the sinking *Hood*, drowned in the Iceland sea with the saddest and craziest and lousiest songs that were ever written in the history of the world rolling over and over in the barrels of their heads.

"Do not ask me to explain the fleeing soldiers who were found shot to pieces with their packs full of impossible pictures of big rubber women all legs and breasts and red underwear and big, white grinning heads.

"I do not understand any of the things they lived by, or seem to have died for: these songs, these pictures, and all the interminable series of limericks that they recited over and over every spare moment of their lives. I do not understand the fabulous courage of soldiers and sailors, dying with their minds full of such weird and ugly lumber, and I do not even know if it is courage."

"Their minds are full of high, but unspoken, aspirations."

"If they ever had anything to aspire to," I replied, "it remained unspoken for so long that it finally ceased to exist."

"They died for humor, and good sense, and even for sports."

"That is the trouble," I replied, "for sports. And worse than that: less than that."

"They have not died," said the stranger, "crying out the name of a leader, or of a god, or of an idol. They died for humor and good sense."

Then I said, "Shall I tell you what were the words on the lips of the dying soldiers at Dunkerque?

"One of them was shot down, while fleeing through the dunes, and his last words were:

'Every morn I fill my pipe
With St. Julian, rich and ripe.'

Another one was smashed by some bomb fragments but had time to cry out:

'Guinness . . . good for you.'

The airman in his flaming Hurricane that shoots downward as straight as an arrow into the Essex marshes is saying over and over, 'George Robey, and Jerry Verno, and Stanley Lupino, and Laddie Cliff.'

"The vultures of Cyrenaica are circling around a British tank, half buried in the sand, mad because they can't get in to where the three Australians burned to death crying out for another chorus of the 'Beer Barrel Polka.'

"Further west, the vultures have picked clean the bones of a hundred Italian officers, and left nothing on them but the pictures of Deanna Durbin which each one held in his hand."

"And the Germans?" says my stranger.

"I do not say I ever even tried to understand the Germans. But the English are in a kind of way my own people, and I am supposed to be able to know them. What do I care for the Germans, dying bravely with their heads full of algebra, potato soup, camera lenses, incomprehensible jokes, rectangles, unexplained hatreds and fears? They are different enough from me so that I am merely sorry when they run head first into their dumb death, but I am not tortured by the inability to understand them. I take that inability for granted. But the English are supposed to be almost like me. Do I have to die, tomorrow, murmuring the names of buck-toothed English movie stars and the slogans of several hundred different kinds of beers?"

"How do we know what you will die for?" said one of the strangers. And the other one said:

"Perhaps for that typewriter, and for the things you write with it. To die for that would be as absurd as to die believing in Bovril and Oxo."

But I answered:

"I just happen to be writing, at the moment. Writing is not my life."

"Did you not come here only to write? Was not that your purpose?"

"No, that was never my purpose. I came here looking for a person: and while I am waiting for news, to guide me, I write down everything I know."

"Then you would die for the person you speak of, but for nothing else?"

"I am in the midst of death," I said, "and you know for what reason I am here."

IX

I was at Danecape with the Frobishers when I was fourteen.

The house in Yorkshire was made out of large blocks of
stone and had huge windows. Dim light of the moors! In
the front was a tennis lawn, and in the back, between the
house and the stables, were thick rhododendrons and pine
trees. On still days, in all the pines, the wood doves
boomed and cooed without ceasing, driving everybody
mad. Behind that, somewhere, was a great garden closed in
by hedges, where there were a lot of flowers and some
raspberries. Two gardeners constantly worked there.

For morning prayers, the cook and the two maids, in
their pale blue smocks and white aprons, would come sidling in at the other end of the dining room. The family
knelt, with faces to the wall. Faces in hands, and elbows in
the soft seats of the dining-room chairs. Mr. Frobisher read
a lesson from the Bible and some prayers out of the *Book
of Common Prayer.*

Then the maids went sidling silently out again, and you
helped yourself from the various silver chafing dishes on
the sideboard, where there would never be any ham or

bacon because the Frobishers were vegetarians, in honor of science.

And I would come to breakfast with the smell of the stables still strong in my riding breeches. This was by no means criticized because the stables were part of the education that was to make a man out of an orphan.

The wood doves would already be booming, and the new sun would be slanting through the pine trees and making soft light on the purple hills, full of wet heather, when I was up in the stables with a pitchfork, cleaning out the stalls of the two ponies, under the direction of the two nieces, girls older than myself, lovers of horses, who groomed the ponies without tiring, seriously, cleaned saddles and stirrups, leatherwork and metal, fed the beasts and watered them. When I was through with the fork, I went on working with the brush until my arm and wrist ached. I curried the warm sweet smelling flanks, until the bay pony shone like mirrors and the roan like tropical wood.

As we worked, a portable gramophone, set on a broken chair, ground out little nasal tunes from Gilbert and Sullivan operettas.

I stood in the clean straw, brushing the side of a horse, unhappy and hungry, while the inhuman metal playfulness of the gramophone voice repeated in my ear:

> "To make the punishment fit the crime,
> The punishment fit the crime."

Then, between records, you would hear the squeak of the handle. One of the nieces wound it up again with hefty arm. You would once more hear the wood doves booming, outside in the sunny trees.

Later in the day, we would ride on the stony roads or on paths through the heather. That was our reward.

One learned to appreciate the ride by having to work for it, which was a good enough theory if you were crazy about riding in the first place.

The Frobishers knew, of course, that there never was a boy or girl born in the world that did not love to ride horses more than anything in the world, and it was probably every boy's ambition to be able to go cubbing, and then on a real hunt on a real hunter.

The nieces, in the summer, thought always of the autumn and winter, of the hunting season. And when they weren't riding (exercising the ponies rather than themselves), they were reading about riding in books by a man called Lieutenant Colonel McTaggart, full of little diagrams of the way a perfect horseman conducted himself and controlled his mount.

The nieces were never very talkative: they generally didn't speak at all in the stable except to tell me what I was doing wrong. When Mr. or Mrs. Frobisher had something to say, the nieces listened attentively, with slight frowns of complete concentration, but I remember one of the nieces, after having been drawn out, on the subject, by Mrs. Frobisher, got off a short speech about horses and the relation of the horse and his rider.

"Riding is like good manners," she said with a deep, rustic blush, "after all. I mean manners is putting other people at their ease, and riding means you consider the horse, too. After all, only a cad would yank on a horse's mouth to pull him up: you should pull him up gradually, and also only a cad would gallop a horse downhill; it's awfully bad for their hoofs and their hocks, and they might get lamed for good. Besides, you ruin your own horse. Think of the horse. You're responsible. It's like noblesse oblige."

At first they were tolerant of the mistakes I made in the

stable, and the lack of thoroughness with which I was inclined to groom my pony. They believed that I was slow in
learning, and dull. They hoped that perhaps enthusiasm
would conquer natural stupidity in the end.

But they came to agree that I was showing signs of
complete apathy toward horses. I was slow not merely because I was dense, but more particularly because I was
unwilling. Stupidity wasn't so bad: stupidity is common
and can coexist with a sort of fundamental decency in
many chaps. But not unwillingness. No. I was unwilling. I
shirked.

That would have been understandable. A certain indolence can be condoned in a chap, when he doesn't know
any better: if he shirks a little of his job and just wants the
reward without working for it, it is not commendable, yet
nevertheless natural.

What was not understandable was that I wasn't interested in the reward, either. Not only was I shirking the
task of grooming, but I was also quite ready to forgo the
reward of riding the horse afterwards. That was a pretty
gross trait. There was a lot wrong with this orphan.

Of course, he wasn't strictly speaking English. As a matter
of fact, he wasn't really British, either: it was by no means
certain you could call him a thorough colonial. He was
showing signs of too many bad Continental traits, a kind
of French sullenness, perhaps treacherousness, a kind of
Spanish haughtiness, a kind of Italian indolence.

I began to be observed.

One day they let it be known that I wouldn't be riding.
I agreed immediately, I gave up without a glum look, I
dropped everything and went for a walk on the moors,
through the wet heather, a long way, walking into the cold
wind, to the top of a hill about three miles away, where
I sat on a big stone and looked at the distant house and
wondered what I was doing in Yorkshire, and how long

it would be before somebody wrote to the Frobishers and got me sent back to London.

I did not have to be here. I had relatives in England, as well as other parts of the world. But they were doing my dying father a favor. I was an orphan.

Also, it was not fair to any child to let him grow up with the disadvantage of my kind of Continental traits: sullenness, independence, dislike of systematic games and sports, perhaps treachery and even ingratitude. Added to this was the suspicion of Mrs. Frobisher that perhaps I was also being secretly rebellious, and sulking over the vegetarian diet of the house. As a matter of fact, I didn't care about that at all.

I had hardly even noticed that they were vegetarians until one day I had to see the local doctor, about a cold, and he drew my attention to it.

That was because he had been fighting with them for years about meat and not-meat as a true basis for health.

I could not imagine why the doctor was so pleased to treat my cold, until he got me alone and said:

"Now, confess: aren't you hungry? Don't you get tired easily? Wouldn't you like a good piece of beef? Wouldn't you like a nice steak?"

"I suppose so," said I, overwhelmed with wonder that among the people of this part of the country there might be a disagreement about any question at all. I had assumed that they were all absolutely unanimous about everything, horses, outdoor sports, the trickery of Latin peoples, and also, probably, the evils of meat.

"What do you mean, you *suppose* so?" said the doctor.

"Well . . ."

"Come on, man, are you another one of these vegetarians? Have they converted you?"

(My attitude toward the Frobishers was never quite the same from this moment. The doctor was asking me into

his league against them at least on this one question: therefore they weren't absolutely right in everything they said.)

"I like meat," I said.

"What you need is steak."

"Try to tell Mrs. Frobisher that," said I, catching on
rapidly.

"Believe me, I will."

The result of that was that I was believed to have acted
like a knife-in-the-back Italian. I was thought to have gone
complaining to the doctor with my lies and hypocrisy, that
I was sick for lack of meat.

When it became established that I was sullen, and a
sulk, I began to get systematic sermons from Mrs. Frobisher.

After lunch, one day when I was off to get *The Count of
Monte Cristo* (in French, too) and take it out and climb
up in a tree and read it in the branches where nobody
would go looking for me, she came after me and stopped
me in the door of the library.

"I would like to speak to you," she said.

We sat down, facing one another on small, hard chairs
in a corner of the room. I turned the book over and over
in my hands while she spoke, until she got exasperated
by the movement and told me to stop it, and I put the book
down.

"Did you ever read *The Jungle Book,* by Rudyard Kipling?" she said.

"Yes."

"Do you remember who Mowgli was?"

"He was a boy who lived wild in the jungle, with the
animals," I said. "He lived away from people. He was wild."

The conversation was taking a wrong turn.

"Did he live alone?" she said, introducing her theme,
and before I could say anything, she answered, "No, of
course not. Nobody can live alone. We all have to depend

on one another. Mowgli lived with a pack of wolves. Why do you suppose the wolves and Mowgli got along together? Why?"

She paused. I had my own answer. I said:

"Because he liked the wolves and they liked him. They got along well. They were like brothers."

"First came duty," she said severely. "What duty?"

I thought a while. I couldn't remember anything about duties. I said:

"I suppose I don't remember. I just thought they liked each other."

"Duty held them together," she said, "the duty to run with the pack. The pack came first. Run with the pack. Hunt with the group. Everybody depends on everybody else. Everybody does his bit. Mowgli had his part to play too. It is like the Three Musketeers," she went on, "do you remember what kept them together?"

"They liked each other," I said.

"No," she said, "it was their motto, 'One for all and all for one,' that kept the Three Musketeers together."

I remembered the motto. Then the sermon went on, with a parable.

"Of course you know that the Indian Civil Service is one of the hardest services in the world to get into. I used to know a young man, who was like you in that he knew many languages, but he was also very clever and hardworking, too. However, he had one terrible fault. He sulked.

"Well, of course, he was so brilliant that he got into the Indian Civil Service almost at the top of the list. And they sent him to India, and it seemed that he had made a wonderful career for himself in India. And remember there isn't a man in either of the universities that wouldn't give anything for the chance to be in the Indian Civil, because that shows you are among the most brilliant men in the world.

"But I said this man, let us call him Jones, had one fault. He sulked. He did not get along well with other people. He grumbled. He argued with others. He did not run with the pack. Furthermore, he could not stand criticism; now India is a difficult country to get along in, in many ways, because of the Indian people, and there were many who had been in India much longer than Jones, who had more experience than he had, and only meant to help him when they pointed out the mistakes he made.

"Perhaps they thought Jones was a little uppish, too. It doesn't do to be uppish, you know, even if you are in the Indian Civil and all that. At any rate, they saw this trait in Jones, and they tried to lick it out of him, and get him to run with the rest of the pack.

"Instead of that, however, he sulked more and more, until finally one of the army men gave him a good talking to about something he had done that was not quite proper in India, although it might have been all right anywhere else. Instead of accepting the criticism in good part, Jones flung out of the compound and went off by himself on his horse into the jungle."

She paused and looked straight at me, guessing, perhaps, with how great sympathy and approval for this man I was about to take my book and disappear into the trees.

Then she said:

"And he was never seen again. No man knows what became of Jones. He went off in a sulk, and was never heard of afterwards. Think of it," she said, "that brilliant man, killed, perhaps eaten by a tiger!" Then I went out of the house with my book in my hand and dived through the laurels and climbed into a small cedar with roomy branches where you could sit and read comfortably. And there I read how the Count of Monte Cristo, tied in a sack, hiding inside with a knife, was thrown for dead over the high bastions of the Château d'If into the sea.

Now I walk along the railings of Hyde Park, where the earth is torn up around the battered antiaircraft guns. They see much use.

It is strange to see guns so used, instead of shiny and new. In America, all I saw were pictures of new, clean guns, lined up, supposed to look smart and trim. But England smells of smoke, and the guns in the parks are in the midst of the mud and sandbags of the battle, and everywhere you see buildings with men repairing the roofs or the windows, or buildings that have simply burned to shells and are being cleared away. The city is weary and full of scars. The smoke is everywhere.

I think of the Frobishers' house in Yorkshire: the glass is out of the library windows. Light falls into the fireplace where part of the chimney has been shot away. In the naked dining room, they eat their vegetarian dinner. On the plain, spick and span mahogany table are the little side dishes of raw carrots. But the wallpaper is stained with rain.

During the dinner itself, the carpenters come in and start boarding up the windows. Mr. and Mrs. Frobisher, and the nieces, continue to eat. Mr. Frobisher extends his neck and speaks to his wife with his quiet, ingratiating smile, saying:

"The Germans cannot go on losing all the men they have lost in Greece. I understand there has been a terrible slaughter in Greece, more terrible than in Belgium. Soon we may hear of peace, don't you think?"

Then, when he has finished speaking, he looks from one to the other of the nieces.

One of them says:

"When the war is over, we will be able to go to Norway again."

"And Sweden. Do you remember how we fogged all the snaps I took at Visby, and they were spoiled? I shall take new ones!"

In the silence you hear raindrops clattering into the fireplace behind them.

"Were the tanks out on the moors today?" says Mr. Frobisher.

I wonder where the nieces really are. Undoubtedly they are somewhere in uniform. Just now I had imagined them sitting at the table, sixteen-year-old girls, still, with their round red faces, and their big teeth and their short straight hair, their fierce bangs and their freckles. That is the way they were twelve years ago. A long time.

Even in peacetime, in a certain kind of light, the huge cold rooms of that house in Yorkshire had looked like the rooms of a gutted castle: great gray walls, bare, covered with pale light coming in off the moors through the huge panes of the windows, panes whose glass warped the lines of the gray clouds, slightly, and the line of the hills.

On the long evenings of summer, when the sun might be going down in a series of long yellow streaks between the clouds over the moor, we would all sit together in a little group of straight-backed chairs, in a corner of the high-ceilinged library: Mrs. Frobisher and her husband, the two nieces, and I, we crouched together soberly around a small fire in the grate that warmed the August evening a little.

We would spend an hour or two of waning light listening to Mr. Frobisher read from Charles Kingsley's *Water Babies*, about two chimney sweeps who had escaped from an industrial civilization that I could roughly identify by the cities I had seen, but didn't yet believe in, into a kind of positivistic fairyland that baffled me completely but that, in many respects, resembled this house.

In this fairyland they learned a lot of lessons in utilitarian morality both reasonable and crude: Be nice to others in order that others may be nice to you. There were many sermons, flowering symbolically here and there in the plain gardens of allegory. When she caught me, after meals, Mrs. Frobisher added more sermons of her own.

The one I remember best concerned a problem which I had never dreamed of, because I didn't know anything about evolution.

"We all know Mr. Darwin's theories of the origin of species," she said one evening when she had me trapped in the drawing room, "and we all know the story in the Book of Genesis in the Bible."

I think this woman had once been a schoolteacher, in some progressive school in Scotland, before her marriage. Anyway, I knew what half of her statement was about: the Book of Genesis. The other half she explained to me:

"And yet science shows that all the higher creatures develop out of the lower creatures, that the strong survive and the weak perish. The dinosaurs have died away because they were not equipped to resist the changes in climate that began to come over the earth. Man, the highest of all the animals, is the next step above the ape: we know this by skulls, bones, and teeth. All these things have been found and proved. Science knows man comes from the monkey because he is highest in order, and came last. It is just a question of development. Except for the missing link. Nobody has found the missing link."

All of a sudden, a flash of illumination: I see the waving canvas walls of a side show, in a field, in America, in the hot sun. The grass waves in the heat as hot as copper, full of paper napkins and Coca-Cola bottles. The crowds of men in straw hats, carrying their coats over their arms, and the women with small, cardboard fans continually flapping at their red necks. Children clinging to the sweaty hands of their parents. They all crowd into the door of the tent. And painted on the canvas is a ferocious savage covered with hair, tearing some unfortunate people to pieces in the jungle. The sign says:

"The Missing Link."

"No one has ever found the missing link between man and the ape," Mrs. Frobisher continued, "and yet science knows evolution is true. But since religion knows the Bible is true, how can science be true and religion be true?"

It was a question that had never bothered me, but it was a question.

"It is all perfectly simple," she said. "The Book of Genesis merely says in a symbol the same thing that the theory of evolution says in science. The seven days of Genesis are more than likely a symbol for seven hundred thousand or maybe seven million years, I forget which.

"Yet in the Book of Genesis, which means the creation, the creatures are made in the same order science says they were, starting with the lowest and ending with the highest of all. And there really isn't any conflict at all between Darwin and the Bible: the Bible is the symbol of Darwin's theory, and Darwin's theory is the scientific way of saying how they were all created."

She looked at me squarely, having proved her point, and I moved a little uneasily in my chair, and the thought came into my mind:

"Maybe this woman is a little crazy."

I have still not been able to make out why she brought this up, except that she had decided that I needed an education and a decent English training.

Then I remembered the two lieutenants, and her two nieces, and people like them. I remembered the concentration with which they always listened to everything Mrs. Frobisher had to say, and realized that she was thought, among them, for her vegetarianism and other little whims and all her talk, to be a very clever woman.

X

It is a blue, sunny, misty day, like any day in summer in time of peace. During the night, there was nothing, no noise, no planes, no raid. Then, for the first time, in this quiet, I become aware of the ache of tiredness in my muscles and the stiffness in all the joints of my bones.

I am not tired from exertion, but from a sort of vague, continuous movement, without any real intervals of rest. Sometimes I curl up in a chair for a few minutes, then sleep, then wake up, and go somewhere else.

Part of the day the typewriter is in my room on a table, and I walk around and around it wondering where to begin.

Part of the day I am out of the house, walking in the streets.

Back in the house, Madame Gongora's, I look, again, out of the windows. People pass at intervals on the sidewalk below my window, reading the newspaper, or smoking, in silence.

Outside my room there is a clatter in the hall: it is Valdes, working with a broom and a dustpan, sweeping. He wears a blue canvas apron. There is something wrong with the water pipes: the water in them creaks and coughs all day and all night.

Also, wherever, you walk in the city, the wind blows at you, particles of dust, stone, cement flying around, always, thick. You are always getting things in your eye, as a result of the air raids, because the air is full of small, sharp fragments of the city.

It is the middle of the morning. I have come in the house with dust in my eye. Valdes clatters with his broom in the corridor. Downstairs, amid the heterogeneous lumber in the living room, Madame Gongora drinks coffee and reads the poems of Paul Valéry, sitting in a chair, in the middle of the room. I walk around the typewriter three or four times, then write:

I am in a church, extraordinarily bare and light, because of the plain glass in the windows. The stones are cold and shabby. The varnish on the pews is too dark. Candles burn in front of a statue cheap as wax. The stations of the Cross, along the walls, are in awful, yellow bas-relief.

But the church is full of people.

The beautiful churches, with the fine high arches and the flowering traceries of the windows that once were filled with flaming glass, those churches with the square, fourteenth-century towers, are mostly empty; today is not a Sunday.

Those are the old churches, the beautiful churches, the ones with the sweet, harmonious bells, where, Sundays, they sing hymns and preach sermons. Those are the churches where people come together, with black books in their gloved hands, because it is righteous for people to be together in a place, because it is nice to sing hymns on Sunday.

But these other churches are as cheap as speakeasies, they are bootlegged away in the slums, and are crammed with ugly things, and every day they are full of people.

If they were no more than meeting places of people, no-body would come to them. The people come to them for some other reason, for the presence of something besides people. They come there every day.

On weekdays the beautiful churches, with white spires, stand embarrassed and do not know what to do. Maybe four or five people come to a Communion service. Sun weeps in the big, shy windows of those churches, and the walls cry out faintly, ashamed of their emptiness: until the bombers come, and the roof of the church burns and the blind tower dances in the smoke.

Then all the ministers run out of their houses and raise their arms and shake their heads in grief at the beauty that is dying before their eyes, and return quickly to their rooms and write, in letters to the *Times:*

"The flames that have burned this beautiful house of God will leap across the waves of the world and the whole world will burn with the fires of just revenge on the barbarians."

But the walls that were always empty do not reply, and do not contradict the minister with the memory of their emptiness: they only cough out smoke through all their windows, and the firemen turn white streams of water up into the burning eyes of the building that is being destroyed.

Small bells ring like silver before the altar of this other, crowded church, this church that is half-outlawed by a strong tradition of several centuries. And when the small bells ring, people get up from every corner of the church and struggle among the knees of their companions until they get free into the aisle, and follow one another slowly, in line, to the rail at the altar.

I am in line, with my feet slowly moving up into the place of the feet of a soldier. He goes before me, as the line moves up, looking down at the floor, and I look at the back of his red neck.

Ahead, between the crowded shoulders and over the heads of the men and women, all kinds confused together, at the rail I see the white robes of the priest and acolyte go quickly from one to the next.

Then the soldier ahead of me and the women ahead of him and all the rest of us begin to move forward again.

I come out of the church into the street. The roofs of the houses are golden in the summer's mist. The crowd disperses in several directions at the foot of the church steps. Across the street, coming out of a white-fronted ABC tea-shop, I see B., in her uniform.

"How are you?" she says. "Still in London, I see. Mrs. Frobisher told me she had seen you. She criticized you: she said you were here for some malignant purpose."

"I suppose she did. I am staying at Madame Gongora's. Which way are you going?"

We walk together on the short, wet grass of the park. Over there, in the mist, stand the not too distinguishable guns with sandbags piled around them.

"What have you been doing?" she asks me.

"Trying to find something: I don't quite know what."

"Something to write about?"

"Not quite that. There is plenty to write about, if you just want to cover paper. And yet I am looking for something special to write about, in a way."

"Write about Madame Gongora's bodyguard. I think he is very sinister, and so does everybody else. It is only her influence that has kept him at liberty."

"Valdes?"

"Yes."

"There is nothing so sinister about him, except that he happens to be Spanish. Is it so sinister to be Spanish?"

"I don't know. I don't know why anybody is sinister any more, but I don't like Valdes. I have forgotten how to make general statements. I simply don't like Valdes: I wouldn't say I thought he was sinister for belonging to any kind of a category, like Spanish."

"Are you going back to all the popular feelings against different kinds of races, inferior to the English?"

"I tell you I don't know. But it may be true. If it is, then it is. But I haven't time to think about it. I am suspicious of you, too."

"Why?"

"Because I don't think you care who wins this war."

"That is no way to say it: say I don't like the war, and I wish it would stop."

"If it stopped now, the Germans would be the winners. Would you want that?"

"I cannot argue about the war, or anything else. I do not like it. I wish it were over. Whoever wins, it is going to be very hard. I have no ideas about justice, who is right, who is wrong. I know that a lot of people are being killed."

"Don't you believe the Germans started the war?"

"In the sense that they began fighting it, yes."

"Germany is guilty."

"I don't know the meaning of the word guilty, except in the sense that I also am guilty for the war, partly."

"You? Now I don't understand you."

"I don't understand you, either. I cannot use the word guilty in a sentence like 'Germany is guilty,' because I don't understand the level of meanings on which the word works, in that application. I understand it differently."

"How could you be guilty of a war? Nations are guilty of wars."

"Nations don't exist. They can't be held responsible for anything. Nations are made up of people, and people are responsible for the things they do. I am a person: I can be guilty of wrong, I can do harm, and have done."

"They say Hitler is guilty."

"He might be. Only I don't know enough about it. He might be more guilty than any other one person, but he isn't the only person guilty of the war, and as to saying how guilty he is, I'm afraid I don't know, I don't know. I don't know who's guilty. All I know is, if anything happens to the world, it is partly because of me. That is all I know: my share in it. But I don't even know the relation of my share to all the rest of the responsibilities, and don't attempt to."

"I haven't time to know as little as you want to know."

"It doesn't take time."

"It takes getting used to."

"It depends how much you want to get used to it."

"I don't at all," she said. "I stay up all night, I hang on to the walls and the explosions of bombs break my back in half, I live in black smoke of this city's burning, and the dust of the ruins is always in my throat. I don't want to know that nobody's responsible. I want to know that one man is. I haven't time to know anything less arbitrary than that. Tomorrow I may be dead."

"What difference will it make, then, what political fact you happen to have known?"

"I want to know who is responsible."

"Even if it isn't really true?"

"In the simple sense in which I want to know it, it will be true enough for me: I will have been killed by one of their bombers, and the symbol on the rudder will be enough for a judgment."

"You want to die, perfectly sure of who it is you hate?"

"Yes, why not? At least it is something definite to die with."

"Not definite enough for me, and not the kind of definiteness I want," I said. "I want to die knowing something besides double-talk."

"There is no such thing as double-talk," she said, "not to me, there isn't. Not any more."

We are passing the emplacements of the guns, whose barrels, pointing almost straight upward, shine dully in the summer sun.

Then she said:

"Is that what you are here to find out? Your part in what is happening? Do you want to know how much you yourself are responsible for?"

"You guessed it," I answered her.

Where was it that I first met B.?

One summer in Yorkshire the Frobishers, with their nieces and me, drove twelve miles to the house of a friend, and there we played tennis and had tea. The friend had nieces also, one of whom was B.

B. was as young as I was. That made us the youngest of all the people there. We didn't get to play much tennis, not that we wanted any.

B.'s uncle and his wife and the Frobishers and their two sets of nieces, excluding B., made up several doubles sets in different combinations, and B. and I didn't get the court until everybody was tired, and it was almost dark, and time to go home anyway.

B. was a skinny, quiet girl, not pretty, with straight hair and bangs. We just sat at the edge of the tennis court, embarrassed at being the youngest of all, embarrassed at being classified together, arbitrarily, and asking one another a series of insolent questions about the schools we went to.

There was a fat spaniel, also. He came over, and that made three of us. The dog was too big and too fat and too old and too friendly, and didn't make it a more congenial gathering. B. realized this and kept saying to the dog:

"Oh, go away, you old fool!"

But the dog didn't go away, and he followed us, panting, when we got up and wearily walked about in the flower garden with all our muscles tired from inactivity.

At tea, I got a better look at B.'s uncle, who was a curious little man. They called him Captain. He was round and red in the face and simple, and had a mustache. I couldn't imagine what it was he had been captain of until I found out he had been captain of some kind of a cargo steamer out of Newcastle but had retired from the sea upon inheriting this house.

All during tea, he talked in tones of diffident amazement of what was then the sensation of the day in Yorkshire: the first talkie, *The Jazz Singer*. This was, by far, the most wonderful thing he had ever seen or experienced.

He kept repeating this fact in a weakly challenging sort of a way, because we could all see the Frobishers were sneering at the idea.

Finally Mrs. Frobisher said:

"You are altogether too fond of the cinema."

"If you could only see *The Jazz Singer*," said the Captain, "you would never criticize the cinema again. It is something altogether different. If you could hear those voices . . ."

"American voices, I believe."

"I admit, there is nothing special in the quality of the voices. Really, I suppose it was the songs, the music, the story. The whole thing was moving in the extreme."

"I think you're being a little ridiculous, aren't you?" said Mrs. Frobisher. "This weakness for jazz is a new acquisition on your part, is it not? I don't seem to remember you singing the praises of *jazz* before."

"You wouldn't call it exactly jazz," said the Captain quietly, with a kind of doggedness and shame that did not prevent him from continuing, "The songs were rather slow, more like ordinary songs, not like jazz."

"Well really, if it's called jazz, it must *be* jazz," said Mrs. Frobisher in a huff. "I don't see how you're going to get around that."

"This wasn't jumpy, like jazz. Know what I mean?" the Captain explained, in tortures of embarrassment. "Jazz just goes boom boom boom. This was infinitely more slow, infinitely."

"Oh, very well," said Mrs. Frobisher sarcastically. "We are quite sure the music was delightful. But I still doubt very much if we shall ever find time to go to such a film, or, in fact, any film at all."

After tea, everybody went out rapidly toward the gardens, the lawns, and the tennis courts in little groups discussing the Captain's folly.

"Can you imagine him, poor dear," the Captain's wife was saying shrilly over at the other side of the lawn, "he wept and wept and wept when the Jew sang!"

The Captain himself was saying earnestly to Mr. Frobisher as they came out the door,

"I give you my oath, George, I cried like a child."

"Really," said George with a wide and frightened grin, "really?"

You could see everyone was discussing the Captain's tears. B. said to me, "I saw the picture too, and I thought it was frightfully silly. Did you see it?"

"No."

"Well, don't," she said, "it's awful."

I met her again in the Isle of Wight, at the other end of England, two years later.

I used to go to the Isle of Wight and stay with a friend from school called Andrews.

Andrews' father was a parson and lived in a village rectory. The nearest movie was at Freshwater, three or four miles away over the downs; if you walked it was seven or eight miles around the downs by road.

One afternoon we all went to the movies, around the downs, by bus: the parson, who was a large man with bowed shoulders and small eyes and a face that looked at you, no matter what you said, as if he expected you to make some kind of witty statement, took us all: me, Andrews, and Andrews' little sister Anne, whom I always, for some reason, respected a lot, although she was nothing but a little girl and never said anything much or was of any account at all.

It had been a little dreary all day in the rain, in the rectory, but when we all got into the bus to go to the movies, things became more exciting. The bus swung out of the village and went like mad up the narrow road under the dripping trees. Behind us we could hear the foghorns booming over the quiet sea.

In a very few minutes we were at Freshwater, all getting out of the bus talking and laughing in front of the movie, which at once disappointed me by not being a real building but just a big temporary shed covered with corrugated iron. As for the film itself, the posters said it was something very old, very silly. Nevertheless I was still excited.

We did not go into the movie at once, because the parson had to go to a shop and buy a comb and some tobacco and some shoelaces and pencils and a small tin bucket for use on the beach and some Ping-Pong balls and some rubber heels.

So the excitement was still greater when we got into the movie, which had not yet begun. So we sat in the rickety, squeaking seats, surrounded by groups of children. The whole theater was filled with the smell of rainy mackintoshes and wet clothes, and the shrill, expectant, excited voices of children. We stared at the white screen.

The parson would lean over, once in a while, and say something funny, and his son would laugh with a great deal of satisfaction at what his father had just said. But the little girl Anne just looked solemnly at the screen. And all of a sudden, I was overwhelmed with sadness, sitting at the end of the row, because I suddenly remembered all the times I had sat in movie houses at the beginning of the afternoon, waiting for the picture to start.

It was like remembering my whole life.

I had spent all the days of my childhood with my legs hanging from the hard seat of a movie, in a big hall full of the sound of children's voices.

I remembered the dim lights, the gray arching ceilings, the red signs saying exit, and always, in front of us, the big white screen framed in black, but still dead, inanimate, flat, hard, waiting for the dark when it would become alive, transparent, full of movement, people, and adventures.

It was as if, now, instead of remembering all the movies, the illusions, I remembered only the waiting, the reality, the facts of the theaters I had sat and waited in, for the beginning of the afternoon show.

Now, instead of remembering the live pictures on the screen, I remembered all the dead decorations in the dim-lighted theaters: the gray muses that lolled and smirked on top of the phony arch over the proscenium. They were the worst of all creatures, painted as decorations for a place that only fulfilled its true functions when it was all in darkness and nothing on the walls or ceilings could be seen.

I remembered domed ceilings peopled with distorted, half-draped figures among painted clouds, extending their stubby arms in the gestures of rhetorical flight: all asking to be swallowed up by merciful darkness.

I remembered walls painted up with marble columns on a flat surface to fool the eye, with the illusion of horrible balustrades over the top of the proscenium arch, leading into distant nightmarish illusions of impossible Italies full of gypsies with timbrels. Beyond it all, a distant Vesuvius, fabricating smoke.

"I really hope it will be a good picture." Nobody under-

stood why I said that. Of course, everybody always hoped
it would be a good picture, naturally. Only the little girl,
Anne, felt as serious about it as I, because she said immediately and with great earnestness:

"Yes, I do too."

The film, however, was so bad that none of us could
stand it, and neither could any of the kids in the place who
began to fight among themselves out of disgust and dis-
appointment until the place was too full of noise for us to
hear any more what was being said in the deep tunnels of
artifice behind the screen.

We left in the middle of the picture and came out into
the rainy street, blinking and confused, like sick people,
horrified at the pallor of one another's faces, at our unnatural expressions of weariness and dismay—as if the
movie had been so awful that it had destroyed our health.

Then, while I was still dizzy and still could hardly see
properly, I saw another group of people coming out of another door, and in the midst of them a girl with pretty eyes
and white skirt, still slim, but a lot changed: it was B.

I spoke to her before it occurred to me that she might
not remember me. But she did. We talked together shyly,
not particularly friendly, either, as though we had last
seen each other not more than a month before. I made a
bitter joke about the movie, and when we introduced each
other to the people we were with, it was less like an introduction than a sort of explanation of who we happened
to be.

Instantly, as soon as the names were mentioned, the
people B. was with knew who the Andrewses were, and the
Andrewses knew who they were, since they all lived on the
island. B. and I remained, strangers. But in a second we
went away again, each with the proper group.

At once Andrews began asking me questions.

Who was she? Where did she come from? Did I know her

very well? Did she live in Yorkshire all the time or just sometimes? Where did she go to school?

The parson said, "She must be staying at Admiral Mayhew's, since those are the Admiral's granddaughters."

So then we were invited to go to Admiral Mayhew's house for a fancy dress party.

The parson, who had no car of his own, hired a taxi for this, and we all went to Admiral Mayhew's, by night, in the rain.

We all got out of the taxi and ran up the steps into the big lighted door of the house, and took off our coats and revealed our disguises. Andrews had got a brown friar's habit from somewhere (he said he was a monk). I had borrowed a pair of riding breeches and boots and a sombrero someone had brought back from a cruise to the Antilles and South America and said I was a horse thief. Anne was dressed in a big hoop skirt and said she was a shepherdess. She had a crook, too; not, however, an eighteenth-century wig. This was just as well: better that she should be a shepherdess with her bobbed, dark, child's head of hair.

At first we didn't see B. anywhere, then she appeared in a crowd of people.

She was dressed as a gypsy, which was very inappropriate for her fair skin and her guileless, blue-eyed face, but it was an obvious costume when you were in somebody else's house and had to make a dress up in odd skirts and scarves.

I asked her to dance. She came away from the group, and we started across the floor together immediately aware that neither of us was a good dancer. Twice she tripped lightly against the toe of my shoe.

I made a couple of jokes about costumes.

When the music stopped, I went into another room, where some older people were standing around a table and leaning on a mantelpiece drinking whiskey or wine. Some stranger dressed as a pirate (there were plenty of pirates) told me to help myself to the port, which I did.

I stood in the room with a glass of port, slightly apart from the group of grownups. I heard a red Indian chief say to a Regency beau, "It's the damn moles. They ruin everything, as usual. It's high time to put out traps."

Then I put down the glass with the red sweetness of the wine still sticking to my lips, and walked out of the room again.

Andrews, as friar, was sitting on a step halfway up the staircase with B., as gypsy.

"I said, "Hello," from the bottom of the stairs, looking up. They both turned their heads at once and said hello and then turned again to one another and went on with this conversation I could not hear.

I walked through the doorway and looked at the dancers in the other room.

It was just a big ordinary room with grayish wallpaper. The rugs were rolled up and there were chairs along the wall. The place was full of white electric light and of people in inappropriate clothes, dancing to the music of a gramophone.

I was suddenly very embarrassed and ashamed to be there. I was embarrassed by the number of cowboy hats I suddenly perceived, dancing decorously with eighteenth-century ladies and gypsies. I took off my sombrero and held it in my hand, much aware of the silliness of wearing my hat in the house. I was ashamed of my own disguise, of the riding breeches and the riding boots and my swagger that had been most of the costume anyway. I was most ashamed of the title of horse thief.

It was very humiliating, all of a sudden, to see so many awkward, innocent pirates, so many very young cowboys,

so many childish gypsies, and to realize that perhaps I myself had actually walked into the house believing I was a
horse thief. And then I became even more embarrassed to
think that there could be no reason for being a horse thief
except that I must have anticipated that there would be a
hundred cowboys there, and I wanted at least to have a
different and somehow opposed character.

I went away from this room also and hid my sombrero in
the room where all the coats were, and took off the scarf
that hung around my neck, probably like a boy scout's,
when it was the right way around, and sat in a chair in
what must have been the library, scarcely less unhappy,
now that I looked like nothing more than a person with
riding breeches on.

But while I sat there wishing the party was all over, in
came two serious men, one in eighteenth-century costume,
another merely in a dinner jacket, and the one in fancy
dress (who turned out to be the admiral) said to me:

"I'm awfully sorry, old chap, could we ask you to move
for a moment and let us have this room to talk in? I'm
sure there are some nice girls without anyone to dance
with."

The word girls he pronounced "gells."

Andrews and B. were no longer sitting together on the
stairs. The empty step they had been sitting on hit my
heart with something of the impact of a bomb. I stood in
the hall. Looking to the right into the lighted room where
the men were drinking port, I saw Andrews. Behind me, the
parson backed out of the coat closet, holding all our rain-
coats. He said to me:

"Are you coming home with us or do you want to stay a
little longer?"

I gasped, "A little longer," and did not even wait for
Andrews to start putting on his coat. I hurried into the
other room, where B. was standing by the window all

alone. I paused for a moment and looked at her to make sure.

Yes, she was bored to death.

Then I knew that I loved her more than the whole world, and we began to dance.

XI

JOURNAL: LONDON

Piccadilly is like a street that has been submerged for not more than twenty-four hours in the sea.

The top has been blown off the Sandeman's port sign, halfway down, by a bomb fragment: leaving about half the letter "S" and the rest of the word.

The main difference is that there are sandbags around Burlington House, there are no cars in the street, there is dust everywhere, everything seems to be under repair, and there are people in uniform, men and women, walking in rare sparse groups, with their heads down, in a hurry.

The street is like a person that is ill. The same features that were once healthy are still there, only, now, full of weakness, strain, and confusion.

But perhaps it is only like the face of a person who once seemed healthy. Now I look in the weary, overwrought features of the city and wonder if the sickness was not there when I knew the place before, an illness not yet openly declared.

I think of the foggy nights in Piccadilly, five years ago. The complacency of the night!

The whole city was like a big, quiet room, filled with no

separate, violent traffic noises, but a universal, muted rumble, from everywhere.

It might not even have been night: even in the middle of the afternoon, the streets were filled with the vast complacency of night. Signs glowed in the quieting fog, and the outlines of the buildings were lost in the upper darkness. The windows of the shops glowed like bright and friendly aquariums.

Men in bowlers and dark suits, bowing a little, forward-marched in and out of the quietness with their rolled-up umbrellas. Men full of propriety, calm and proud, neat and noble.

But the vast discreet silences of the city were all false.

The huge discretion of the fog was hiding everything and was hiding too much.

The whores in ermine marched out of the doorways, in the dark. Then suddenly you realized that the fog was hiding the cries of thin clean men dying of dope behind many thicknesses of the walls of flats. Then suddenly you began to suspect, inside the reticent houses, long, inarticulate insanities. Then suddenly you wondered what perversions you might read if you knew how to interpret the windows where the curtains seemingly slept, they were so still.

Now I walk in the street by the light of day.

They have cleared away the glass and bricks from the last big raid, and the street seems tidy again, but it is a bombed street.

The place where they dug out a time bomb, in front of the Ritz, is still boarded off, but there isn't any traffic anyway.

What they can't clear away is the dust and grit that flies, thick, in the air, from the ruined places, the wounds in the rows of buildings.

Then suddenly I realize there are some women not in uniform, not in military uniform, standing in the same old places, along the streets: the whores.

They are dressed for the war, in slacks and turbans, and to a stranger they would look like smart, rich women, the London whores, in their dark red trousers, young and defiant, beautiful, not ugly. They scan the street like cats and call out to the officers and the airmen in several languages.

"Ola, halte tu, cher senor! vin nossotru, lis elegantis, per voir li jolis amourade, vin con mi hasta mi happy casa! Halte tu, offizir! Arreste, caro aviador!"

And one cried out to me as I passed:

"Y tu aussi, tu joli estranger! Vin comigo, seas mi companao d'unios momentis di solacion, mentre manana todos estaremos mortos!"

I go on down the street without the laugh of fear and derision that used to yawn in my entrails when the whores called out to me in the old days, when I didn't know the difference between life and death.

Behind me, I hear a man speak to one of them in a phony rasping voice:

"I believe you are the bravest girl in the world. Come with me and tell me your life story and I will buy you a drink."

I turn to see who the man is. He is dressed in a business suit, and helmet, and has gold rings on his fingers and looks like a banker. He is probably a famous writer.

There is a line at Fortnum & Mason's, for the expensive foods: strawberries and peaches higher than caviar used to be. And, standing in the line between an airman and a lady whose picture was often in the *Tatler*, but whom I can't remember, stands Madame Gongora's bodyguard and servant, Valdes. He looks pretty dangerous with a bowler hat on.

He is the only one in the whole line with a gas mask

slung over his shoulder, and it disturbs me to see this character singled out in such a way.

Here is a man thought by many to be an international spy, if only because he looks exactly like one. If he were the only one in a crowd without a gas mask, I would feel safe from gas. But he is carrying a gas mask.

Seeing me, he tips his hat. "Bonjur, signor."

"Bonjur, Valdes. Ke faz, ici? Emplettes? Comprados?"

"Li madame mi faits comprer fraises, melons, groseilles, ananas, en soma, muchas frutis varios, para lis entretenimientos ci jour por la tard: ha invitat molto genti a dinieri."

"Frutis," I exclaim with a laugh, "cela costara un joli pfennig!"

"Dijistid verdaz, cierto, signor!"

At the sound of our speech, people in the line turn around with very suspicious looks, so I break off the conversation and say, "Well, so long, Valdes."

He cries after me, with a loud, solemn, completely un-English:

"Gut bai-ye, signor," which rings and re-echoes all around the walls with the awesome false friendliness of a spy. People in line begin to whisper to one another, very excited. Valdes remains at his place in line, calm, solemn, with his gas mask over his shoulder.

I go up the steps of the ARP center, where I hope to find B. As soon as I get to the open door, I become aware of danger: something has happened.

The hall, in front of me, was bare and empty, but in the back of the building could be heard the rumor of some commotion: also I smelled smoke.

I went into the first door to the right, into the room that had once been the drawing room of this nobleman's town house and was now stripped bare, bare of everything. There was here nothing but the white walls and the naked floor and a telephone, tied by its wires, standing on the floor in a corner. It was as if the place had been sacked by communists.

From the door at the back of the room, gray smoke came, fairly thick. The place was on fire. I could hear a commotion of feet and a man's voice shouting:

"We'll all burn to death!"

Then he came stumbling out of the back room, cursing and holding a handkerchief over his face. He shouted behind him to someone, "Well, for heaven's sake, look sharp and get the fire extinguisher."

I wondered whether to run to the telephone and shout into it that the ARP center was on fire.

I heard someone run out into the hall from the door of the other room, where the fire was. It was a woman in uniform, who presently came bustling through the door with a small Pyrene fire extinguisher in her hand and an exasperated expression on her face.

"Come on, look sharp!" said the man.

"Now you don't have to be so shirty about it," she answered and went into the room full of smoke.

"Place on fire, eh?" I said.

"It's a wonder we aren't burned to the ground. This is the fourth time in a couple of months."

"What happened?"

"It's always the same thing. Those girls throw their lighted cigarettes into the wastepaper baskets and walk out of the room and the next thing you know, there's a fire."

The woman came back from the inner room and said:

"Well, it's all over. There was absolutely no need for any fuss at all, Mr. Robinson. It's all over."

"Someday we'll all be burned to cinders, thanks to you," said the man. "Some of you young women are more useful to the Nazis than to anybody else, I'm sure!"

"Don't be so disgusting," said the girl.

I asked where B. was. The man said she had gone out somewhere, but he was sure he didn't know where. The girl said, over her shoulder, "You'll probably find her in the Berkeley."

I found her there, in the amber light of the cocktail bar, a room with a disturbed atmosphere, as if the painters and plasterers were working in the next apartment and were going to start in this one tomorrow.

She was sitting at a table with a noisy group of young women, some ARP wardens, like herself, one a nurse, one in an ordinary, plain street dress. There was also a skinny, tired-looking naval officer who, as I found out upon speaking to him, was drunk.

I sat down among all these people, whose names B. told me, vaguely waving her hand around the table, and shook hands with the naval officer, the rank on whose sleeve meant nothing to me.

He was the one that was talking, in scarcely comprehensible speech:

"Of course I tell you, these things were not exactly unsuspected. Quite natural of course. Couldn't talk about them before this for the best reasons of security. However, you can bet your old hat we knew. To begin with, the air arm knew. Well informed, air arm, called the eyes of the fleet. You know, in modern war, eyes are the vital organ: organ of sight. If you can't see, well, you might as well be blind. The air arm's very sound. Lots of tips and hints in the past week. For instance, the information can be given out now, no importance whatever, past and gone."

No one at the table looks at me. I see one of the nurses looking at her fingernails, and feel the things I swear she is thinking about me.

"You're a stranger, old man," says the navy man, "but even if you are Hitler himself, which doesn't seem to be at all the case, all this is old stuff, you understand. But we knew last week; we were actually in between Jersey and the mainland, almost in sight of Granville. The hotels on the beach. Big hotels which I remember as a child, when I had the opportunity to visit Granville. You know, summer hols."

"What happened?" said the nurse.

"Precisely. What happened? Nothing. Precisely. Nothing. The whole place might have been dead. Knew right away. Not a thing flew over us, only the birds.

"Didn't take the air arm to tell us," said the naval officer. "We could see for ourselves, it was quiet enough to go ashore and have a swim off the beach. Nearly did. I loved that place, you know. I assure you, I was full of the tenderest sentiments, old Granville.

"But apart from all that rot, I suppose they just left a couple of platoons there and sent everything east. Then the reconnaissance came back with the most fantastic stories. Can be told now, of course: wouldn't be letting out anything."

"What, for instance?" said the nurse.

"Half the known aerodromes were completely cleaned out, not a plane left, all got out: hopped it. We knew right away something was up. Of course, there were still a lot left behind, you know, enough to keep us busy ourselves. Then the same story began to come in from Libya, too, you know. Right away we guessed what was up."

"Of course, there were all those rumors in the paper, but you didn't know what to believe."

"But we knew," said the officer. "The air arm, the eyes of the fleet, had smelled it."

"Anyway," said B., "I'm glad."

"You," said the nurse, "poor B., and you used to be a communist."

"Don't be absurd."

And then I began to guess what they were talking about.
"What happened?" I said. "Is there something new?"
"Of course," said the officer. "Germany has gone charging into Russia, now. Fantastic, isn't it?"
"I think it's splendid," said the nurse, "now that will give us a bit of a chance."
"No doubt, no doubt at all. Give us a great chance. But isn't it amazing, though, the different combinations allies can get into?"
"Yes," said the nurse, "I suppose they're our allies now, if you look at it that way."
"Absurd, isn't it?" said the naval officer, drinking his brandy and coughing weakly.
"That doesn't prevent me from hoping they slaughter the Germans and get slaughtered themselves."
"All I know," said B., "is that whenever I think about politics I get a little sick."
"Why? Everything's as it should be," said the nurse. "Things have finally worked themselves out so that they're *just!* The Germans were meant to fight the Russians in the first place, everybody knows it. When I think of the thatched cottages of Kent burned out by their bombs, and all the delphiniums in their gardens destroyed, when I think of the Centre Court at Wimbledon, where so many famous tennis players have played tennis, and the North Stands at Twickenham, where so many famous rugger players played rugger, and when I think that all this useless destruction is nothing but a horrible muddle, a kind of insane joke of kismet, as you might say, then I really wonder if justice means anything. But there *is* justice. Everybody knows the Germans and the Russians were supposed to kill one another off in the first place, and now they're at it. *Finally!* I hope it lasts a long time, so that they'll do a good thorough job on each other!"

"Hear hear," said the naval officer, "and so say all of us, what?"

"Well," I said, "you must excuse me, I have to go."

"Imagine it!" said the nurse as I was getting up. "I heard from my sister in Buckinghamshire that the guttersnipes had actually bombed a kennel near Amersham full of dogs that had been evacuated from the cities! Sometimes I feel the sufferings of the innocent animals and the flowers more than those of the people. I hate to see a rose garden, for every time I do I think how horrible if all the lovely plants were blitzed!"

B. got up, and we started away together, and the nurse was saying:

"Perhaps they will finish each other off in short order, and leave the world free for decent humanitarian people to live in."

"I admire your idealism, really I do," said the naval officer, "but you mustn't forget, you know, that the Germans are terribly strong, and the Russians may not put up any kind of a fight at all."

"Touch wood," said the nurse, "but I hope the Russians fight until the last Nazi and the last communist is cut into little pieces."

B. and I walked through the lobby and out into the street. Men were already collecting the garbage and dumping it into a truck.

XII

In front of Madame Gongora's house is a car, a Bugatti. Valdes is filling the tank, pouring petrol through a funnel, out of a large drum. The petrol is clear in the sun, I smell the sharp smell. The air is bright. I am very happy, all of a sudden, to see a car getting a tankful of fuel, on a nice day like this one.

"Que se pass, Valdes! Hay petrulio! Brav!"

Valdes laughs.

The house door opens, Madame Gongora comes down the steps, clashing with bracelets.

"Hola, Madama!"

"Caro Mertoni! Bravo Dia!"

"Ou se vado?"

"No importa."

It appears that now, in the garage, there are fifteen drums of petrol. Where from? Who can say. But anyway, she has all this fuel. She puts on a pair of sunglasses. Her black hair is bound up in a white turban.

"Venga," she says, and races the motor.

All the way to Hammersmith Bridge people look up curiously at the lone, fast car, racing down the streets, in and

out of the barriers around the places where the street is
torn up, swinging out past the army lorries here and there,
and the buses, and the horse-drawn carts.

In Hammersmith Broadway, a line of soldiers working
on the street flies past us like a row of fence posts, all
turning toward us in great curiosity, a blank curiosity without friendliness or hostility.

I begin to remember all the things one used to pass on
this road out of London: the pub called the Oxford and
Cambridge, and, on the other side of the bridge, the pub
called the Boileau.

The bridge is utterly empty. We race across it in the
middle of the road, and the white river winks through the
cables that flash by us on both sides.

It is low tide, and the blue mud shines along the riverbanks. The trees beside the reservoir dream in a kind of
warm haze.

Before we are off the bridge, I have looked back, over
my shoulder, at a place on the bank, where B. and I one
time stood jammed in a great crowd on a moored lighter
to see the boat race. Now the river and the riverbanks are
wide and empty in the sun.

"Pobre Mertoni, que pensador, ce jorn-dui? De que
pens? Del pasado?"

"Ese pasado que no posso comprendi!"

"Triste?"

"No, Madama! Mais confusissimo! No tengo parola pour
esprimir las memorias idiotas que me convengon together
nella cabota, pero estupidois like the reunion of the old
boys' clubs of all the schools put together."

The Kingston By-Pass is wide and empty, and I watch
the speedometer go up to eighty as we go down the middle
lane of the concrete road.

The motor sings in my ear no louder than a radio warm-
ing up. The road shines like silver. The wind flaps in my

ear like flags and the gay voice of Madame Gongora talks about the world.

I watch the tiny, wobbling needle on the dashboard. Ninety. Ninety-five!

The sun flashes on the green hill.

Madame Gongora begins to sing a flamenco song about the world:

"O Mundo! Tus frutas relucen como hierro,
Y tus frumentos como cuchiles azules,
Y tus fuentes como las diamantes pequeñas
Que queman los ojos de los niños andaluces!

Todos los relojes del mundo me preguntan
Con sus estupendas voces de plata,
Porque los edeficios miran en el aire,
Porque los árboles esperan la llegada
Del amoroso viento, campeador."

She is saying that the harvests of the white world shine like tin, that the flowers in the fields are no less bright than drops of metal, that the woods this year are silver with the fruit that shines like water, and that, caught in the cages of the Spanish orchards, the angry sun booms like a pigeon, but with the coming of the wind, the apple trees will rustle like a child's dress.

She says that the world is full of the speech of metal clocks, and the sun ticks in the timeless trees. She says the clocks are more solemn than the children, but that the stars are no less prompt than the wires of our guitars.

She also says that she has seen the light crawl higher in the big speedometers of the buildings, but that a red geranium appearing in one of the middle windows put to flight the metallic numbers that were nesting in the walls like starlings.

She says that the world is nothing but perspectives, like

empty streets going off in every direction. At the end of the longest street there is an iron railing and, beyond that, space.

As soon as the buildings look at the sky, they fill with the rattle of adding machines; they are counting up the stars. Yet the real way to find the lost planets is to sight your telescopes along the edge of childhood.

When the sky grows pale and the lights in the windows of the banks go out like radio dials, the cities will be full of the gramophones of day; but when the sky darkens and the lights go on in the windows of the all night factories like objects, it will be safer if the city sounds as childish as the prayers of birds.

O Mundo, tus relojes cantan como los números cardinales,
Y tus palacios nocturnos no se duermen,
Apasionados de la geometría
Pero las huertas lloran,   ·
Mirando las sangrientas caras de los palacios
Y las carreteras! sinvergüenza Mundo!
Ya se mueren de hambre.
¡O Mundo–O–O–O!

Then suddenly the car swings over the brow of a hill, the wide country seesaws down and up with space full of fields, trees, lines of identical houses in the sun. Five or six, or more, antiaircraft guns march off leftward all pointing at the southeast sky, now full of clouds white and pretty like in an eighteenth-century landscape painting. The gunners stand against the sky with their helmets off their heads and their arms folded.

Ahead of us the road is full of barriers, armed men, an officer, motorcycles. The road is closed where a bomb fell. The brakes of our Bugatti grab tight inside the wheels and we cry out down seventy or eighty feet of road to a hard stop.

The man in the helmet comes over slowly.

"I say, didn't you see the sign back there?"

We didn't see the sign.

"You can't drive up here, you know."

We do not speak. Madame Gongora smiles.

"Where are you going, may I ask?"

"On the Portsmouth Road," says Madame Gongora. When she speaks English, her accent is strongly foreign.

"Would you mind showing me your license?" says the officer.

Just out of hearing the two men in uniform talk over the paper she has given them. I look at the camouflage on the guns, I look at the sky.

A row of idle soldiers along the ridge stare at the car, and at us in it.

The officer comes back.

"Will you come with me, please?"

We both get out and follow him off the road. I feel, under my feet, the field grass. We walk a little way up the hill to a house. Already, before we go through the open door, I can see, framed by the door, the officer who sits inside at a table.

We wait, while our man talks to the one at the desk. We hear the superior officer say:

"How do I know?"

The other beckons to us to come in.

"Where are you going?" says the superior officer after studying us a while.

"Out on the Portsmouth Road," I answer.

"Not you," he says. "I am asking the driver. Madam, where were you going?"

"Out on the Portsmouth Road."

"Where? What town?"

"No town. We were just driving."

"Why, may I ask?"

"Because it's a nice day."

The officer coughs and shifts in his chair, and looks up at his subordinate, a little embarrassed, as if that seemed a perfectly good reason, to him. The subordinate says:

"Their tank is full of petrol, sir."

"Oh," says the superior. He is still embarrassed. Nobody says anything.

Then the superior officer says:

"Have you any other identification with you?"

Madame Gongora takes, from her handbag, a passport and other items which I do not recognize, and hands them to him.

"After all," he says in a not unfriendly tone, "there was a sign along the road that said you mustn't drive up here, wasn't there?"

He looks at Madame Gongora's passport, and then, reflectively, speaks to his subordinate:

"I say, has there been, at any time, a country called Casa involved in this war?"

"Not that I know of," says the subaltern, "but then, I don't know half these silly countries."

"Casa is not in the war, on either side," said Madame Gongora.

"I just thought it might be one of those places Hitler took over this spring, but perhaps not." He hands her documents back. Then, to me:

"Can you identify yourself?"

"I have no papers with me. Only a letter I got this morning from America. I left everything else in London. I'm not a British subject either."

"Who are you, what are you? Passports don't mean much to me either. I can't tell one from another. I'm not a pass-

port inspector. Tell me who you are, and what you're doing here."

"I'm a writer."

"What do you write, novels?"

"I am a poet. I write a diary. That's about all."

"That tie you have on," says the officer, "is that a Clare
College tie?"

"As a matter of fact, it is."

"Very good. Then you went to Cambridge. Who was
your tutor, at Clare?"

"Telfer," I replied.

"Oh yes, Telfer. That's right. I went to Emmanuel, for
my part."

"I had some friends in Emma," I say.

"Oh yes? Who?"

"C., M., F., G., D."

"Don't remember any of them," says the officer, "never
ran across them. About fifteen years after my time, anyway." He continues, "What did you do at Cambridge?"

"I visited the proctor, in his rooms in the new court at
Magdalen, and paid him a fine for not having a square.
I had tea with some girls at Girton, sitting under a tree
in some fairly long grass, in the untidy part of the grounds.
I had a friend who grew a beard. I read some of the works
of the Divine Dante. I was gated for ten days in the Lent
term, for being drunk. I did cartoons in the *Granta* and the
Gownsman. I sat in the writing room of the Union and
wrote short, boastful letters to my younger brother, and
from the library of the Union I borrowed Cocteau's *Thomas
l'Imposteur*, Stendhal's *De l'Amour*, and Flaubert's *L'Education sentimentale*. I came home with a girl in a punt
from Grantchester and it got so late we left the punt halfway up the river and ran to the nearest road and took a
taxi to town. I had a friend who hanged himself in the
showers at Clare. I had many friends with pianos in their

digs, on whose pianos I played, badly, 'St. Louis Blues.'
I lent somebody my copy of *Ulysses* and never got it back.
I had my fortune told by a gypsy at the Chesterton fair,
whose tent was later overturned by some friends of mine
from Trinity Hall. I wrote a poem that was refused by my
college magazine, *Lady Clare*. I thought the Loch Ness
monster was funny. I went to see French films at the Cos-
mopolitan Cinema. I liked the Lion best of the pubs."

"Did you sit in the Baron of Beef with riding breeches
and a checked cap?" said the officer in command. "Did
you go to the races at Newmarket? Did you own any
horses? Did you shoot duck?"

"No," I replied, "I did none of these things, but I fell
asleep on the last train from London and didn't wake up
until Ely. I had a friend in St. Catherine's who was afraid
of his tutor, Chaytor. I ran up a big bill for cigarettes which
they gave up trying to collect. I signed a petition for an
expelled communist to be reinstated in the London School
of Economics. Once I forgot to go to a garden party in
Trinity Hall, and right after the party was over I met the
don who had invited me in the street, and didn't recognize
him. I was invited to tea by my Italian supervisor, and
came one week too early, when he and his family were just
going out somewhere else."

"Did you ever throw a brick through a shopwindow?"
said the officer, questioning me further. "Did you ever get
arrested in Huntingdon for riding on the running board of
a car through the streets? Did you ever climb into the new
court of Clare over the bicycle shed? Did you ever enter
a public amateur competition in playing the drums at the
Rendezvous dance hall?"

"Yes," I said, "I confess to you that I did all of these
things, and also that I bought a copy of Plutarch's *Lives*
(Dryden Trans.) in Heffer's and went next door to the
Lion and left the book there and never saw it again. That,

on the other hand, I omitted ever to return to the library of the Société Française an anthology of modern French poets. That I didn't like Marlene Dietrich in *Song of Songs* but that I several times went out with a girl who was known all over Cambridge as the 'Freshman's delight.' "

"Did you ever," continued the officer, "steal a policeman's helmet, get drunk on whiskey at a bump supper, play darts in an inn in Trumpington, associate the mill at Grantchester with Chaucer's 'Reeve's Tale,' and remember, in connection with the millpond at that same village, Lord Byron? And furthermore did you connect Grantchester Church in your mind with the so-called poet Rupert Brooke?"

"I did not do one and three of this series," I replied, "but I admit all the rest. I also spent hours leaning out of the windows of my digs watching the bicycles go up and down Bridge Street. I also admit that my digs were in a house Queen Elizabeth had slept in. I also admit I tore my dinner jacket, climbing over the fence of Jesus College. I also admit that I had, on the walls of my rooms, the following pictures: Van Gogh's *Fishing Boats*, Cézanne's *Mont Sainte Victoire*, Gauguin's *Women on a Beach*, Manet's *River at Argenteuil*, all reproductions: as well as two signed etchings by Reginald Marsh, and photographs of the following persons: N., M.(i), and M.(ii)."

"Anything else?" said the officer.

"Nothing, except perhaps that I saw, at the Festival Theatre, every play presented by the repertory company in my freshman year as well as a program of West African native dances and the Marlowe Society's *Anthony and Cleopatra*, but I was unfortunately gated the night Louis Armstrong appeared at the New Theatre. I might also add that I took part in several scavenger hunts, was twice photographed in the street by itinerant photographers, but never went to any of the May Week Balls."

"Very well," said the officer, "that's good enough. And,"

turning to Madame Gongora, "I believe I have seen your photo in the *Bystander,* so you are identified also."

Then the officer gets up from his chair and follows us out into the sunlight.

"I would offer you a cigarette," he says, gallantly, to Madame Gongora, "if I had any. But I have none."

"Won't you accept one of ours?" said Madame Gongora.

"Thank you, I think I will."

He takes one, I refuse. The subaltern, with bad grace, lights a match.

"Allow me to show you around," says the officer to Madame Gongora. The subaltern coughs, violently, and I catch him, out of the corner of my eye, making gestures of disapproval.

"A pleasure," says Madame Gongora. The officer gives her his arm. The subaltern rolls his eyes in despair and stands back. I join the officer and Madame Gongora, as we walk, in the sun, toward the battery of guns.

"Frequently," says the officer, "I take advantage of these quiet moments of June (for we are scarcely active at all, this week) to muse on my experiences as an undergraduate at Emmanuel."

"Cambridge," he continued thoughtfully, "I am constantly there in spirit. Gray Cambridge, I am in your quiet streets, I sit in my old room, the window of which is a perfect square, and through it still I see the quiet perspectives of the college garden, and a wall, and the geometry of housetops and chimneys farther away.

"Your memory, old Cambridge, shines in my precise mind as clear as a triangle, and here in the time of disorder I make up all the new mental structures from minute to minute, of my life, upon the base of your abstract isosceles peace.

"My three Mays on the river above the weirs make one polygonal experience of order, and the three whole Lents

I lived in my room full of logarithms, form three lucid and concentric spheres that turn around and around without the most abstract whisper of discord, but all the time murmur the harmonious names of Newton and Kepler. Yet the bells of St. Mary's sing to the stones of winter one word, 'Quantum, Quantum,' many times over. I walk in the geometric courts of all the colleges, for in my mind the university is a map full of lovely straight lines and rectangles.

"Moreover I am still keenly aware of the areas of every court and the brittle buildings are to me as clean and interesting as cubes, varying in their capacities for receiving light and air.

"Water slides under the Clare bridge, with the sound 'Euclid.'

"The early setting sun in winter glitters in the pools of ice, among the trees, along the Backs as bright and childish as the quadratic equations of my tenth year, but the high stars among our low, and in no cases distinguished, towers talk to me with great depth, like the curvature of space.

"Cambridge, Cambridge," says this officer of artillery, "you shine still in my mind with the cleanliness of mathematics, as holy as the name of science sounds when it is pure and abstract. Cambridge, you are to me as calculus, with which I was more drunk then than now with gin."

We are approaching the nearest gun.

Behind us, in front of the house, the subaltern stands, with his hands hanging, looking after us.

The soldiers sit in the shade of a tree and under a net of camouflage laden with leaves and grass and rubbish.

Then I speak, also about Cambridge.

"Cambridge, you cry out to me from the past like the waiting rooms of dentists, you swear in my memory like the gas geysers with their big copper tanks heating a shilling's worth of hot water for a bath.

"You look in, forever, to my mind the way ten o'clock in

the morning comes through an unwashed windowpane on the grayest days, and the eyes of your tradition make at me still the green and fragile and dim light of sixpenny gas mantles under a globe.

"Oh, peering Cambridge, I taste you in the broken skin of my lips like the bloody leather of a twelve-ounce boxing glove. I constantly hear the dried scraps of putty falling from your windows onto the linoleum floor, I smell the awful cleanness of soap in the dank showers underneath the College Buttery, where the soccer player hanged himself."

The thought of Cambridge takes fire, feverishly, in my mind, like the things that appeared to be cakes of solidified oatmeal they used for lighting fires in the slick grates of Clare New Court.

"The thought of you empties like old gin out of a glass that has been standing several days, among the clean plates.

"You are as pompous in my mind as the framed, paling documents certifying that the landlady's husband was one of the war dead (1914–18): such documents hang, like the lithograph portrait of the old queen, in the darkness of hallways.

"The wind sings in the shadows of Senate House passage with the sound of a vacuum cleaner, and rain falls on the roofs of Caius as ominously as the motors of a bus.

"The bells of a big Victorian church cast down in the midst of Station Road, the ringing of their artificial past; these bells, neither new nor old, pretending to be very old!

"The bald, scared houses grow along the narrow Cam beyond the railroad bridge, among their own turnips; and Cambridge fears the country all around it, bare as steel.

"The sun falls on the stone of King's Parade and colors it like the parchment skin of dying protestant bishops, but the voices of the different Victorian additions to the colleges make no more noise than clothes.

"Yet everywhere, Cambridge, your real voice speaks as weary as the imitation heroines of the worst films made in Elstree, and rings forever in my mind like bravery and pathos in an empty theater.

"Cambridge, you are as quiet as teashops but as blue as clinics, and I will never forget the town girls' starved laughter ringing along the narrow gutters of the Cury.

"Cambridge, you are as restrained as postmarks on a letter, but you are as disquieting as syphilis or cancer."

Now the officer is taken up with his battery, in which Madame Gongora is also extremely interested. They barely wait for me to finish what I am saying, before he is pointing out to her the new guns, explaining, in detail, their operation.

"I should be interested," says Madame Gongora, "to see them in action."

"Not much action, lately," says the officer, looking automatically upward, "not since they took on Russia."

Out to my right I can see the fields sweep down to a row of pale-colored suburban houses, stretching without a gap for half a mile. Beyond that are roofs, and trees, and more roofs. I see power stations, and churches, and Richmond Hill, and Kingston, beyond which the Thames valley lies under a light haze.

Going over the landscape again, I try to pick out the places where the bombs have fallen, but they are too far away to distinguish. It looks as though one of the power stations was hit.

There is a sound of motors very high. It is heard, quite suddenly, and goes quite rapidly away. The planes were there and gone in a minute. Nobody stirred, around the gun emplacements. Some looked up with their hands shad-

ing their eyes. I couldn't catch sight of the planes themselves. But the officer said:

"Spitfires, from Brooklands, probably."

I look in the direction of Esher. I can make out Sandown
Park Grandstand, at the foot of the wooded hill, and wonder if that race track is being used as a fighter station too.

As we come back past the house, the officer is talking
about all the new radio devices they have to detect the
enemy. Madame Gongora is absorbed in every word he
says, asks extremely pertinent and technical questions.

They go over toward the car. I turn again and look once
more at the landscape, in its new context of war.

The landscape, in its new context, is more completely
comprehensible to me than it ever was in my childhood.

When I used to ride to school at Ripley on the Green
Line Bus, or in Aunt Maud's car, after vacations, or week-
ends, the landscape had seemed without harmony, in
a state full of contradictions. I did not understand these
houses, those distant power stations, nor the dialectic between disorder and all the confident techniques behind
disorder.

I did not understand the relation between idealism and
ugliness.

I always understood the landscape in terms of something else, what the landscape had been once, or what
the technicians dreamed it ought to have been. I could
never see what it was, and I believed it was temporary.

This battery belongs on the hill, a mile from the Ace of
Spades roadhouse (at the crossing where they have carefully taken down the signs that said Kingston, Surbiton,
Norbiton, Putney, Roehampton, Croydon, Leatherhead,
Dorking, Esher, Weybridge), where the small, shiny open
cars of what I thought were crazy rich drunkards used
to stand, in my late childhood.

These guns belong within sight of the distant gasworks,

and race tracks and football stands, and they are part of this view of cheap houses that radiates everywhere from the tired Georgian façades that seemed to be lordly and fine, once, on Richmond Hill. There is no more disunity: they are all part of the same complex problem. So I have found out something I didn't know when I was fourteen.

It took the German air raids of 1940 and 1941 on the suburbs of London to make me believe they existed and were permanent, not just a mistake made inadvertently by builders, and ready to be changed at a moment's notice.

When this was a landscape at peace, I read the signs of the dog kennels, looked in awe and envy at the Ace of Spades, looked at the sky above the lines of new houses, did not comprehend the late Victorian gasworks, nor the electrified suburban railways, nor the motorcar factories, nor the tennis courts, nor the Methodist chapels, nor the football stands, nor the fast cars.

In time of peace, I believed in trees, and fourteenth-century churches, and lawns, and commons, and eighteenth-century houses.

I thought everything else was temporary, and a mistake.

Now there is a war, and I know that the vast suburbs are not temporary, because it takes so much to destroy them, and maybe this disorder is permanent.

The gasworks are monuments like the cathedrals, and maybe they will last longer: and if they are destroyed, maybe they will be rebuilt, only worse: and the landscape was once incomplete without the antiaircraft battery, but now that has made all the rest finally comprehensible.

But even before I turn away from the sight of the suburban hills, to go to the car where Madame Gongora is still discussing all the secret weapons in England with the commanding officer, I can hear the subaltern telephoning, inside the house, unaware that I am just outside the door.

"Yes," he is saying, "a man and a woman. I'll give you

the number later. I said a Bugatti, yes, a Bugatti, over-flowing with petrol, high-powered."

He listens.

"Well, here it is: the woman first. Italian or Spanish. I'd say twenty-eight or thirty. Good-looking in an Italian or Spanish sort of a way. Black eyes and hair. About five foot two. Slim. A sort of a red dress. Yes. No cameras. No. Saw everything. What? He's telling her all about the detector now."

Then he pauses.

"The man: well, about twenty-six, light hair, blue eyes, says he's a writer and went to Cambridge, might be German or Norwegian or Russian. Talks a little like an American. Doesn't smoke, like Hitler: probably doesn't drink, either. Doesn't like Cambridge, although I'm sure I can't say if that indicates anything. Didn't look at the guns, only at the general layout. Probably make a map of it in a minute. Got all that?"

But even before hearing this I had begun to move away. Madame Gongora was in the driver's seat, and, as I started toward the car, she switched on the ignition.

As we swung around in the road, I saw the commanding officer waving, to us, good-by, while the subaltern walked out of the house as if we would certainly see some more of him, but under different circumstances, and in some other place.

XIII

JOURNAL: LONDON

For once, B. is not in uniform, but wears a dress. She is something like herself, the way she stood with folded arms in the crowded green interior of Queen's Hall when we went to some promenade concerts; the way she leaned her elbows on the tablecloth at Pagani's, and smoked; the way she sat curled up in a chair looking at *Vogue*.

Her hair hangs down to her shoulders.

She says she feels sick from sleeping so much more than usual, as if her body could not stand rest. She says she feels sad and tired in a dress. As soon as she put on soft clothes again, she wanted to cry. Everywhere we go, in the parks, she looks for flowers, and if it were not prohibited, if we were only in the free country, she would have already picked armfuls of them.

The Germans have gone away from England, to fight Russia, and the air raid wardens get time to wear dresses, and to sleep a little, and to lie on the grass and remember who they used to be.

The bombers are temporarily away. The antiaircraft gunners are in the movies. The firemen and roof spotters are reading spy stories, or writing their reminiscences, in a hurry, before the raids start all over again. The soldiers are playing cricket, or smoking under the trees, or learning the saxophone again by the correspondence courses they had to drop in such confusion last autumn. The military police ride, in large chartered buses, to beauty spots on the north and south downs where they play catch under the trees, and pick flowers, and drink tea in the thermos bottles of their June picnics.

The sailors spend silver money in the shooting galleries and peep shows of the beaches. They ride with their girls on little ponies, on the sand. The Tank Corps officer walks, holding by the hand, his little son, and the commander of a destroyer carries his little daughter on his shoulder under the marquees of the cinemas.

Only the airmen sit and smoke without speech, in their full kit, with parachutes strapped to their backs, amid the splutter and din and steady rage of bombers, the wind of whose propellers drives back upon the hangars the fine, dry smoke of dust from off the floor of aerodromes.

But wherever B. and I walk, through Kensington Gardens, I know there is behind me a man in plain clothes, like a peacetime detective. Twice I have looked back in the last ten minutes, and he is now, that I look back the third time, yawning and leaning against an empty birdbath. B., also, has seen him.

"Everybody suspects you," she says. "You are being followed, now. I wonder why they haven't arrested you already."

"They had no reason to: they are beginning to have one, though. As long as I am at Madame Gongora's, I am safe, because of her influence. But since I am her friend, I am suspected, because of her mysterious activities, her accent, and her connections with everything suspicious."

"Though I know you," said B., "even I was suspicious of you: for why should you come back here, to write in a diary? Perhaps I no longer am suspicious of you, now, because I am wearing a dress and am a girl, not a half-soldier, awake all night in the noise and smoke and death of the air raids.

"It was not until I dressed as myself, and remembered who I was, that I remembered who you are also: I had forgotten that you were my friend, or that I had friends, any more. But when I am in uniform I do not know friendships, only kinds of fierce, mechanical associations, and animal strife.

"When I am in uniform, I sit and laugh with a thousand men who say they love me, and we talk back and forth and laugh like iron strangers, and drink drinks as bitter as metal, and all our speech is without equivocation, but without any content, either.

"I do not know how many of these men are dead. I do not know where they come from or where they go, but they buy me drinks, or I them, depending who has money, and we call each other friend until there is another alert and we go to our various stations, and I never make love to any of them, but they may kiss me with their harsh or their scared or their vain or their ridiculously accomplished and practiced sensualities, and then I drive them away.

"But when I wear my own identity I remember, without understanding them, the too crude, too gentle, too shy, too savage, too experienced kisses of the officers and soldiers and airmen, and wish their talk had had in it some sort of equivocation after all, because I am tired of the routine of pessimistic frankness, and the cynical loves of the airmen who say they only want you because we are all going to be dead in the morning.

"But when I dressed in my true clothes, I nearly cried, because I wondered if it were a lie that I had ever lived anywhere but in a world that loved machinery, and destruction, and necking by the half hour in a Bond Street doorway."

We walk among hedges. Behind us, where we walked before, when B. was saying what she has just said, comes the detective, with his hands in his pockets, upon the open grass.

Our footsteps ring on the asphalt walk.

"Did you know all these things before the war?" I ask her.

"I could guess them, but I had no opinion about them, even some curiosity. The persistent and studied love-making that the world seemed to believe in, I believed in, because I did not realize how persistent or how studied it was. Now it is part of the war, of which I am tired."

And we walk, and come out of the hedges again, with the detective about twenty yards behind us, loafing along, a blade of grass in his teeth. The gardens are no longer as carefully kept as I remember them, and the grass is less scrupulously cut.

B. says:

"What will you do? Go away from England and come back when the war is over?"

"I have no ideas of what the world will be like when the war is over, or what I will do; I had too many ideas about what the world would be like when the war came, and the war was different from what I thought, in strange ways which I came here to try and understand."

"But will you go away?" she says. "Please go, before the Germans come back. I don't say this because I fear your death, but simply because you are my friend, and for the sake of my own self-respect, I would be happy to have a friend somewhere where there isn't so much of the war, as if there were part of myself, off, somewhere, in a reasonable place."

"There is no reasonable place. The war is everywhere."

"Yes," she said, "but not the way it is here; everywhere people have made the war in their own minds, and everywhere is the mental confusion of the war, but here is also the material as well as the psychological reality, and the two together are unbearable; they are like the objectification of death, and hell."

Behind us, the detective pulls out of his pocket a pack of cigarettes, lights one, and flips the burned match over a hedge.

"When I was in my uniform I was angry with you for being here," she said, "now that I am not, I am ashamed that you should be here. The newspapers are glad when the official Americans fly over to look at us, and wave their hats at us from the middle of a bombed house, but I am ashamed of everything the newspapers are proud of, in this war, and I do not like to be seen by anyone who ever knew me or loved me, when I am in that uniform. Not unless they also are changed into some uniformed thing themselves. But you are not, you have come back here, not as a soldier or a writer for the newspapers, but as a crazy poet. If you had come back as an airman, I would have made you make love to me. But you have come back as a person who has no place in wars, and I remember that you are not an airman, but a person, and I beg you to go away from England, because you are my friend. If you had come here as an airman I would have wanted you to stay until the day you died in the air. But you have not come back as an airman, and rather than have you stay here another day, I would see you die and be in peace, at once."

Behind us, the detective pauses as we have paused, and, idly, stands throwing pebbles into a pond of lilies.

"I can only understand what you say," I tell her, "as a sign of your own goodness, because I am unworthy of all the implications it makes about me."

"Why? I only said you were my friend."

"But so well, that to be the friend of the person who said it in those terms would require more value than I have."

"What are you thinking of?"

"The officers and airmen you speak of."

"What about them?"

"I am in no way superior to them because they fight the war and I try to understand the war. Their pride is no greater than mine, and they are no further than I am from the Kingdom of God. Suppose you believe, as I do, that the war is, in some way we cannot understand, a retribution for the acts of men; my life has probably been much worse than most of theirs." She answers: "Yet what I say is only that you are my friend and they are not; I like you, not them. You love me more than they do, because when you talk I see, in your eyes, the thing you talk about, but when they talk, I see in their eyes something as false as their words, but entirely different from what they say. You love me because in your speech you create things to give to me, but they hate me because in their speech they set little, feeble traps, to catch me, and fool me, and make me ridiculous before the vanity of their scared lusts."

We walk slowly onward. The yawning detective behind us swings his arms, grabs, with his quick hand, at a fly, but misses. I think of what B. has said: it is hard to speak.

"But when I used to love you," I say to B., "not, now, in the theological, but in the narrow sense: I loved you also the way the airman loves you. As a schoolboy I wanted to be what that airman is, and for you I was covered with imaginary uniforms, for you I died upon the field of rugby in a gallant sacrifice, for you I killed upon the field of cricket like a Spanish prince, with fury and abandon. When I was photographed as oarsman, as hurdler, and as thrower of javelins.

"And most of all, like the airmen and the subalterns that have made love to you with their brave sad wit by the light of the air raids, I also never thought of anything so much as impressing you with the experienced way in which I made love.

"Not only that, but like them also I never spoke to you anything but the same pattern of lies and bad jokes, and everything I said was rehearsed, and had been rehearsed not for you, but rather for Miss Joan Bennet, Miss Merle Oberon, Miss Lillian Harvey, Miss Annabella, and Miss Greta Garbo.

"Besides, even though this may be the same for everybody who ever lived nine months of the year locked up in a boarding school, yet I made the worst speeches of all, imagined the most fantastic situations, won the most absurd athletic honors, in my imagination, and was the greatest and most dashing of all the airmen.

"Therefore, when you compare me with them, now, I cannot speak for shame, because I remember the way it was when I myself made love to you."

Our footsteps ring loudly on the asphalt. Twenty yards behind us, the detective, with his hands behind his back, kicks at a piece of paper. B. says:

"If that was true, I was too young to know it then, and whatever you said was false that I did recognize, I did not much think about, because I knew it was false in everyone else as well. But that was in the old days. I am talking of now, because I no longer understand the old days, or no longer even know them: I only know the present.

"And all I am saying is you are my friend because I like you, and I cannot talk about it much, and I only found it out today when I changed into these clothes."

XIV

The officers who were here the other day must have made away with a letter I wrote myself from America. Fortunately, I had another copy. As it is one of my chief documents of identification, I reproduce it here in full:

Mon Cher Caro:

Pendant que vosotros sitzen among the ruina bombarbiert, nosotros, or we others, promenade upon our narrow, gusty New York crosstown streets with our hands clasping and unclasping on the sweaty pennies in our pockets and wonder concerning the problem of communication with the people whose addresses we have forgotten in England, not to mention Occupied France.

Es un problema, hombre! Tu penses, what a heap of crude beginnings I have made on this scrap and that of my cheap letter papers, and all I have torn up and tossed into the heap of papers that accumulate under the washbasin in my temporary room, for want of a wastebasket.

How do you talk to the people you can't even clearly imagine any more? It is nearly as formal and as trivial as communication with the really dead, the dead themselves, the cheap and disappointing and meaningless little messages you get in séances.

Caro Alberto: How is it in the other, astral, world? Are you happy? How are the cornflakes where you are? Are you in a draught? How does it feel to be practically nothing, you poor, white, transparent, squeaking thing? Rap me a couple of raps on this seven-dollar table, if you can hear what I am saying through the telephones of my vest. Who are you with, there, in the nothing? Is that old Aunt Body stirring the curtains, clicking like a couple of teeth?

I have been reading letters and letters from England that have taken up the back pages of the Sunday papers, and the messages are all as vague and as trite and as meaningless as the replies of astral relatives, scratching on a table with their thin feet, the color of spit, in a dark room somewhere, a dark room in a typhoid house in Brooklyn.

"Yes, it is I, Albert.

I am in a bit of a draught, but I like it.

Aunt Walter is here. Her feet are all well now. She complains of the draught too. Feels the cold a little. Asks after Henry. Make Henry take his medicine, she says. It worries her, she knows Henry isn't taking his medicine."

Clink. (Sound of a falling medicine spoon.)

"I, Albert, am now quite different from the Albert you used to know. I am about as light as a horsehair, but have no material consistency whatever, any more. I look, and feel, rather like the reflection of a glass of water in a window. I think I can be worked out by algebra, but that makes me neither more happy than I am now, nor more unhappy."

"Is there anything you particularly miss? Anything we can get you?"

"I would like more than anything else a good game of cribbage."

But, O fortuna tan lacrimos, before the cribbage boards

can be brought in, the sick shade of Albert is frightened by something, by a button, by a ring, or a match flame, or something, and disappears with a squeak into the great beyond, not to be coaxed back until months after.

It is this problem of communication that prevents me from enclosing, along with this letter, a whole packet of correspondence for the people whose names and addresses I have forgotten.

My Dear Mr. ——:

"I do not remember you and you do not remember me, but maybe you lived in one of those big gray houses, square as boxes, along Castlebar Road, Ealing. You had a white mustache, a bad leg, and asthma, and all day long you read the novels of Stanley Weyman. You walked with a cane. You had neither dogs nor cats in your house, and I entirely forget what it was you retired from, but you had retired from one of the professions. At your tea table, where the silver was spread out over what appeared to be several thicknesses of tablecloth, you ate many thick slices of bread and butter and much plain cake, slowly, and talked about the Boers, about Mafeking, about Lord Kitchener, about the Indian Mutiny, to your quiet wife. Your name had several initials in front of it, and several more after it, and I wouldn't be surprised if you belonged to a Royal Society.

"But in the hall, over the umbrella stand, was a copy of some blue and white tile plaque, by della Robbia, and facing that was a picture of you younger, with a dark mustache, not white; with great pads up to your knees, with a striped cap on very straight, with batting gloves on your hands and your cricket bat at rest, in readiness, in your crease where you have taken up your stance, to guard your wicket, you, in the eighties!

"Where are you now, old sir, when the bombers have come over Castlebar Road with more than the noise of the Uxbridge busses, and shocked your gardens with more than the sound of cricket bats knocking a ball to the leg boundary, and shaken the copies of the della Robbia and the old yellow photographs right off of your walls? Where are you now? I do not remember you and you do not remember me, either, and it is impossible for us to communicate with one another and yet I am terribly preoccupied with the question of your possible death."

How would I write to that old man to ask him if he were dead? How would I write to hundreds of other people whom I scarcely remember, who no longer remember me? How would I start a letter to any of those schoolmasters?

"Dear Mr. B.:

"You, with your degree of Master of Arts from Oxford, came riding slowly through the shadows of the elm trees on your bicycle, wearing on your head a cap which looked too large. You turned your face this way and that at the fields, and held up, sharp as a bird's bill, your nose and scanned with your eyes, through the thick lenses of your glasses, the banks and the hedgerows. You were a small, thin man, but calm, and a teacher of Latin. You used to play the piano and sing in a thin and unpretentious voice, but correct, and sometimes humorously.

"And when you got off of your bicycle, you walked a little bowlegged, I think.

"You were a man without anything false or pompous, no pretentiousness, no embarrassments, no vanities, no acting, except for, now and then, a silly gesture, something impromptu that was always funny and pleasant and friendly and always appropriate. That was the best thing: whatever you did or said was not an act to impress the students, or confuse them, or to defend yourself against them, it was not a bid for flattery, it was simply appropriate and good-natured and right.

"Without any bluster, you taught us Livy. To those who took Greek you taught Greek. You sat at the piano in the drill room while all the school was crowded on the benches to practice carols, and it was you who coached us in acting some scenes from *Henry V*.

"I remember, most of all, an act of great and excellent generosity on your part: that I met you by chance some-where in London, during a vacation, and you took me to see a Harold Lloyd movie, where I nearly fell out of the balcony, laughing.

"I think of the rectory in the country where you boarded when you were teaching us. I think of the long rows of houses facing the green, at Ealing, where the din of the Great Western trains, rushing, out of sight, down in the cut, out of London, could be heard: that was where you really lived.

"I can no longer say whether I dreamed those houses were destroyed, or whether I really read it in the paper, or whether I heard it from someone. Even if it were possible to write and ask you if you are still alive, even if it were possible to write such a letter, where would it ever find you?"

All these are letters I cannot write, because I fear to think of the strained and embarrassed and false answers I might get. Those answers would tell me something I want to know, indirectly, but too indirectly, and not in any good way. For the letters that are written from England are filled with an inexpressible content that can hardly even be guessed, all hidden in the terms in which we used to hear from the seashore, or the country, or the relatives away on a cruise.

"Our cities are dreadfully sunburned, this year, with the bombs of the G——s. The roses will not bloom, I think, since there is nothing in the rose garden but a hole. This has been a provoking spring. Of course we have everything we need, jams and marmalades, tea, the works of Dickens and Trollope, woolens, and the ARP posters brighten up the walls here and there. We think it is so sad, unutterable, the disappearance of historic spots; the loss of spoons, old pewter, carpets, coats of arms, family portraits, alderman's regalia, wainscotting, the historic bats and pads of the great cricketers, and valuable collections of stamps and autographs.

"Bound volumes of the *Tatler* and the *Illustrated London News* have gone up in smoke, and my old *Punches* with the Du Maurier drawings arc ashes. So is the Ovid I had in school and my rowing blazer from Baliol; thousands of valuable watches have been destroyed; I have scraped up a few fragments of some of the gramophone records I played in school.

"Father went to the club and it had vanished. They have also severely damaged the North Stand at Twickenham, and everybody is afraid for the tulips at Hampton Court."

So, just as I have never dared to enter into conversation with the spirits of the dead, who appear to worry interminably over lost shoes, mislaid frocks, neglect of small duties, and numberless minute private and prosaic questions about the dull world they have left, I cannot even dare to write to any of the people who have become strangers to me in the bombardments of England. Therefore, I write only one letter: this one to you.

It is to say that they have made another Time Capsule, like the one they filled with scraps and buried at the World's Fair in 1939, with instructions not to be opened until 6939. But this time capsule is an improvement over the other: it is not to be buried at all: but to be left above ground for its contents to be looked at by everyone. It shall not be hidden in the earth, at least not until absolutely necessary. Perhaps the minute before the invading army of barbarians appears, it will be quickly sunk into a deep shaft in the earth for safety, and, perhaps, brought up again when the coast is once more clear. But at any rate it will be above ground until it becomes absolutely necessary to hide it in the earth, with all the symbols of our culture, the tokens of our mysterious life.

I am afraid of the Time Capsule: and of the things that are neatly compressed into it like vitamins into some kind of a pill. All the things the Time Capsule contains will only carry on, for thousands of years, the dreadful, futile, and trivial worries of the dead: that same concern over the lost mate in a pair of shoes, over a dyed dress, a torn stocking, a broken piece of furniture, over Henry's medicine.

I stood in the crowd, at the dedication of this instrument, terrified by the nightmare in my mind of future, Martian scientists, creatures of H. G. Wells, carrying off the Time Capsules, in 6939, through the mists and swamps of the future, as carefully as unexploded torpedoes. But while I thus meditated in my hopelessness, the dedicating official, whoever he was, began to speak:
"Lucky Citizens: Ladies and Gentlemen:

"We are gathered together today to witness what I may well describe without shadow of contradiction as the dedication of a time capsule.

"Europe is considerably weakened, the very moment I speak, by a barbarian's onrush. Self-supporting America, though returning happily from the harvests of democracy with arms full of wheat, cocks a weather eye to the east, takes in hand needle and constitutional thread to make that stitch in (nine-saving) time lest we be caught fallen between two stools.

"But this here capsule I may safely say is nothing else but a kind of bird in hand worth two in the bush full of isms: all our signs and tokens are squeezed in here somehow, lawks, don't ask me how; all by means of science, though. This is a kind of container, if I may be so bold as to make a startling metaphor. What it contains is ourselves, yes, people, ourselves, our thoughts, whether cheerful or glum, our impressions of joy or of gloom, our simple expressions of our homely ideals, our severe picture of facts, our opinions, for whatever they are worth, our pictures of ourselves: just folks.

"All this goes to make up a cordial mental handshake to the future generations long after we have slipped away peacefully with our skin full of drugs and our eyes shining like in the motion pictures.

"Not marbles nor the guilty condiments of princes shall outlive this expensive Time Capsule, and all the pretentious cultures of past ages will turn to dust before our simple, honest, sincere, and unaffected collection of these little indicative facts of our time. No, not marbles shall outlive these copies of *True Stories,* all recorded in tiny pictures of microfilm, for the future generations, assuming they got one of them machines for looking at microfilm!

"Have you ever asked yourself what you would put in your Time Capsule (for eventually every family will sink a capsule of its own in the barren earth of their back yard, no longer any use for the growing of living plants), have you ever asked what little souvenir of yourself you would like to have dug up in 6939: think of it, *you,* five thousand years from now, that same, unassuming, unimaginative, pathetic, miserly, envious little hypochondriac that you are, dug up as a present to the future, your own simple gift to mankind, the unembellished snapshot of your completely unimportant self! How would you like to be looking? Have you thought?

"Well, you don't have to think. In this case, as in every other case, just imagine that the thinking has already been done by somebody else. This Time Capsule contains everything that we are, all that we are proud of, all that, perhaps, we should be a little ashamed of, except that we just aren't because we're simply too honest to be ashamed of anything, aren't we?

"Yes, here are pages of pictures of our big, stupid, dyed-haired girls with their faces bursting open like fruits and their great meaty bodies half breaking out of their bathing suits, and how the future will wonder at the contortions and the stupidity and the pouched eyes and the smeared mouths of our inexpensive lovelies of today! We have left out nothing, no trait whose sacrifice would dub our portraits incomplete: no, we are a generation of Cromwells, we insist on the painter showing our warts along with our great natural beauty: hence, along with the, perhaps popular style art of *True Stories,* we have also the facts of our time: there are, on this microfilm, reproduced pictures of a recent murder in all its regrettable, but lively, horror.

"There has also been packed in this amazing instrument a small box of perfumed grease used widely today as an under-arm deodorant, as well as some of our more popular medicines; a photograph of last year's winners of the National League and American League pennants; pictures of beer-drinking female bowling champions; drum majorettes; a description of an electric razor; a description of the treatment of diabetes, and a collection of Burma-Shave rhymes, such as are enjoyed by millions along our brand-new highways.

"By these, the future will know you as you are; for after all, what is a modern human being but a collection of objects which he possesses and is proud of? You are a pair of glasses, a little bridge of iron teeth, a watch, a tiepin, a belt, a secret bandage of rubber, a box of tooth powder, a half-empty pack of cigarettes, a lighter, twenty-seven cents, a class ring, a pair of shoelaces, a tiny box of aspirins, and clippers for your nails, and a card giving the address of a psychiatrist, and, on the back, the name of an oil to prevent the falling out of hair.

"All these and more things exactly like them are here

inside this little metal marvel, by virtue of a miracle of compression which I cannot hope to explain."

With these words he pressed an electric button of some sort, music began to play through a lot of electric machines everywhere, flags broke out, the people stuffed their mouths with popcorn and the Time Capsule hung in the view of all, from a kind of a cable ready to be lowered into the earth at some indefinite time in the future, but meanwhile, until the coming of the barbarians, on display.

XV

When I wake up in my room at Madame Gongora's, I hear, somewhere, a clock ring, lightly, five. I believe it is the small, ormolu French clock, ornamented with its pair of fancy muses, that stands on the mantelpiece downstairs.

This clock has been stopped by two air raids, and each time repaired. Now, it rings five, lightly, in the darkness. In the daytime, because of the rumor of the city, I would not be able to hear it.

I usually get up at half-past five, when, in England, at this time of year, it should be fully light. However, they have all the clocks in London running on super-daylight saving, two hours fast, so that now it is only three, and I am moved back to the point where I am getting up almost as early as the Trappist monks, who begin the day in the churches of their abbeys at two, with the Little Office.

I look at the dark room, and at the half-light coming through the window. I can see the house across the street, sullen and awake, brooding with its windows open, while inside, the people sleep. Or perhaps there is nobody inside, except a caretaker, or a servant. The people are away, or sleeping, but the house is awake.

I begin to dress, in the silence of three-fifteen.

I go down the front steps of the house. The street is abandoned. I begin to walk.

I am going toward Oxford Street.

Listening to the sound of my own steps, I cross Oxford Street. The next time I look up, I am once again in Welbeck Street.

I look at the Banks on the two corners. I look down into the silence behind the area railings of Number Seven and wonder what has become of the thin, dishonest-looking man who used to come and open the door when one rang.

I look at the big black 7 painted on the pillar at the top of the steps. I know what the hall is like, inside; the floor is a hard-sounding black and white checkerboard. The hall is dark, lighted with the light of mist. You go up two steps and come to the elevator. The caretaker took up strangers, but if he knew you, you worked the elevator yourself.

The elevator started up slowly, and as you rose in the shaft you could see through the windows in the doors the dishonest man walk across the hall to the window seat by the street door and light a cigarette. Then everything disappeared, and you stood, alone, in the rising elevator, in the faint, clean smell of fog and machinery, the smell of the cold shaft.

I had a good hat, I had gloves and a neat coat, and my school tie and, in my pocket, Players' cigarettes, in a flat, light cardboard packet, when I went up in the lift, coming home to my uncle's flat.

I never rode in that lift without being aware of the way the light yellow Virginia tobacco is packed tight in those neat cigarettes. I never rode up to the flat without being aware of the neat column of theater announcements, in boxes, in *The Times*. I was always aware of the bindings of English novels, of the names of new records, of living artists, of the cinemas where the films of René Clair would be shown. I was conscious of all the boat trains that left for Dover, Folkestone, and New 'aven from Victoria. I was conscious of Paris and London, ..nd not obscurely. I was aware, not abstractly, but in concrete detail, of the whole civilized world.

There I woke up in the mornings of Easter vacations with the quiet light of London coming in the two curtained windows. There was a Spanish maid who every morning pressed your suit and shined your shoes, because the Spanish are great for shined shoes. She took the shoes for shining and the suit for pressing when she left the breakfast tray, on which were a pot of coffee and a very small cup for drinking it, and small pieces of toast. The tray was light and the breakfast no less than I wanted. After I had put the tray on the floor, I would read some part of a novel, maybe Turgenev, maybe Evelyn Waugh.

During the mornings of Easter vacations I went out and walked with my pressed suit and shined shoes in the streets of the West End, believing that the world was neat and quiet and stable; perhaps, in parts, ugly and foolish, but, mostly, a happy place for the subtle.

On those mornings I knew I had in my pocket a couple of heavy half crowns and florins: and money was books, or Duke Ellington records in the mornings, while in the afternoons money meant matinees or movies.

I came home from the Times Book Club or the music shops of the West End at lunch time and watched, out of the windows, the flags on top of Selfridges. My uncle, who walked back for lunch, stood in front of the empty fireplace and lit a cigarette and held it lightly. The speech of my aunt and uncle was light and ironic.

Uncle Ralph (Rafe) respected and mocked the school certificate and the higher certificate, with which I was successively preoccupied: he was interested in scholarship examinations for Oxford and Cambridge, which I took and (in the second case) passed.

I also respected Uncle Rafe because he mocked the House of Windsor, the Frobishers in Yorkshire. I once argued with him for a few minutes that Ravel's *Bolero* was not phony, but soon saw he was right. The next time I heard Ravel's *Bolero*, I knew it was phony.

Now I stand in the street, in the second summer of the war, and look at the area railings, the locked door of this house, where the flat used to be. Uncle Rafe died of cancer before the war. He was in Spain.

The sky is beginning to get light, over the roofs of the houses. It is ten years ago. I come down the steps in my pressed suit and my shined shoes with a packet of Players' in my pocket and my school tie on. I am with Céline, my cousin, who is French.

We have tickets to the new Charlie Chaplin picture, *City Lights*, and we catch a bus in Oxford Street and go to the Dominion Theatre, new and cheap, fancy and concrete, over by the edge of Bloomsbury.

I talk to Céline and for some obscure reason come to the conclusion that she is a lot younger than I am: I cannot think why. Either someone has told me Céline is younger than I am, and I believe it, or else I simply get the opinion she must be younger than I because I am doing all the talking. I ask her for opinions on a lot of things, and she has no opinions. I forget whether we are talking French or English, and whether or not her English is better than my French. It doesn't matter.

Or maybe she just looks younger than I am. Anyway, the picture starts. The name Charles Chaplin comes on the screen, and at once everybody begins to laugh. I forget Céline.

I will always remember the corny tango that was the theme for the blind girl's appearance in *City Lights*, not because I wasn't a little embarrassed by all the blind girl parts, but because I can't forget the picture and the song goes with it. I saw the picture afterwards, twice in Rome, and the song goes with that, too.

It was in *City Lights* that Charlie Chaplin fought (wearing his hat and shoes and white trunks) the funniest and most terrifying prize fight in the history of the world. It was in *City Lights* that he met the drunken millionaire. Drunk, the millionaire thought Charlie was his only friend: sober, he didn't know where this little tramp came from, and had him thrown out, arrested. The millionaire was always getting drunk and meeting Charlie and sobering up and having him arrested.

Once when the millionaire was drunk, Charlie took his car and rode around in it slowly, with one foot up on the door, cruising close to the curb. You watch him going along in the big shiny car. Then you realize he is going about the same speed as a man with a cigar. Charlie is some distance behind the man with the cigar. Going about the same speed, and in the same direction as the car and the man with the cigar, is a bum.

Then the man drops the cigar and disappears around a corner, the bum picks up speed; Charlie, in the car, beats him to the corner, hops out of the car, and snatches up the cigar butt, and, taking his hat off to the other bum, gets back into the car and drives away, sedately, with his foot up on the door, smoking.

The picture is over. The blind girl, with the money Charlie miraculously won in the crazy prize fight, has gone to Vienna and returned, with her sight restored, owing, she thinks, to the generosity of an unknown millionaire. She sees the little tramp standing outside her new flower store, looking, pathetic, at the flowers. He starts to hurry away, she calls him back, offers him a flower. I forget whether she recognizes Charlie when, putting the flower in his button-hole, she feels his coat and remembers. The picture ends with that music. I am not too embarrassed by the pathos of the ending, because the blind girl is so pretty. Anyway it really hasn't got much to do with the scene in the ring, in the night club, in the car, at the unveiling of the war memorial.

Then Céline and I go to the Oxford Street corner house and I am embarrassed to ride up several floors in an elevator just to get an orangeade in a big, cheap, red, eclectic sort of a tearoom.

As it turned out she became a nun.

I don't know how long I have been standing here, in the street in front of the house where my uncle used to live, but someone has walked up to me, around the corner: a policeman, in a metal helmet, like a soldier's.

The clocks strike six. It is really only four.

The policeman says:

"Do you know you are being watched?"

I look over my shoulder. The detective, who has followed me about for two or three days now, is standing in the doorway of the closed bank, with his hands in his pockets. He does not move, but simply looks across the street at me and the policeman.

"It's all right!" I say. "That's a detective."

"How do you know?"

"I assume he is."

"I never saw him myself. He doesn't look like one. Any-way, supposing he is? I should know something about it, shouldn't I?"

"That's your business."

"Look here, I don't know why detectives should be after you, but neither do I know if that lad over there is a detective. And if he is, why doesn't he give me some kind of sign?"

The man stands in the doorway, with his hands in his pockets, without moving.

"Why should he want to follow you?" says the policeman. "If it comes to that, who are you, standing about the empty streets?

"I'm a writer," I say. "I am looking at this house because I used to stay in it, sometimes. I am thinking about the way it was, in this street, ten years ago."

"Who's he, then, if you're a writer? Why are you being watched?"

"He's a detective. Don't you know writers are suspicious characters, just because they are writers?"

"Not at all," said the policeman. "Writers are respected and looked up to in a democracy. My son, who fell at Dunkerque, in his bravery, always wanted to be a writer. Everybody wants to be a writer, in a democracy. I do too."

"That is the only reason I can think of, why they have a detective after me," I answer, "because I am a writer. I go around looking at everything, and that is suspicious. Isn't it suspicious? You're a policeman, you know what's suspicious and what isn't!"

"That man following you, *that's* suspicious. I don't believe he's a detective at all."

"I have no way of knowing," I said. "However, he's still there."

"I'll soon see if he's a detective," said the policeman, stepping down from the curb to cross the street. "As for you," he added, to me, as I was standing still, watching him go, "you can move along. Don't stay here. You have a place to live: go back there. This is no time to be lingering about in the streets, idle."

I start back toward Oxford Street, and as I turn the cor-

ner I can see the policeman talking to the man who has
been following me, under the doorway of the bank.

It seems the man is angry. I can hear his voice, loud. The
last I see of him is an insulting gesture. Then the policeman
grabs him by the arm.

Perhaps, after all, he isn't a detective.

In any case, it doesn't matter at all whether he is or not:
as long as I am no longer being followed.

I turn the corner, and come to the church I am looking
for, and go inside. White light looks at me through the
plain glass.

I am late for the six-o'clock Mass, because I stayed too
long, standing in that other street, looking at the house
where I sometimes stayed in holidays from school.

The priest turns out and faces the people, turns back and
faces the altar. Orate fratres.

I kneel in a pew next to a soldier. There are a lot of
people in the church. But I do not remember how it was in
the Catholic churches before the war, in England, because
I had never been in one, then.

Now the quiet twin candle flames up on the altar talk to
me, in the silence of the Low Mass.

"You who went away from here in terror and confusion,
and have come back again to see the harvest of the whirlwind, why did you return?"

"Because I had learned the nature of my terror, and now
I came to see if this whirlwind had been sown, in the past,
by confusions like mine."

"You who went away from here lost, would you ever have
returned here if you had been lost still?"

"I make this journey for the reasons Dante made his."

"Are you an exile, stranger?"

"Yes, I am an exile all over the earth."

"You who have wanted to return to the midst of this fire

and penance, for Dante's reasons, are you afraid that you are in danger, in this hostile country?"

"I know I am in danger, but how can I be afraid of danger? If I remember I am nothing, I will know the danger can take nothing from me."

"And yet, are you afraid of the danger?"

"Yes, I am afraid, because I forget that I am nothing. If I remembered that I have nothing called my own that will not be lost anyway, that only what is not mine but God's will ever live, then I would not fear so many false fears."

The little bell rings. The people come to their knees. The candles with their light flames speak to me in the silence before the consecration.

"You who fear the words and ideas and opinions of men, you only fear those things because you love them too much.

"It was because of these that Christ was betrayed in the dark streets of London, and it was because of these that you have made Christ's tears and the Blessed Virgin's to be heard without ceasing in Camden Town and Stepney.

"Because you loved too much, in your childishness, the things the world adored, Christ's Crucifixion flowered in London, like a bloody tree, and you, who did not know what it meant, once fled into the edge of darkness with a cry.

"You lived in a world where pride had long been burning underground like a fire smoldering for a hundred years in a caved-in coal mine. You lived in a world where, for despair, the young men hanged themselves in the showers of colleges. Your pride was not the world's fault, but yours, because you were the one who finally consented to be, also, proud. Look now where the Crucifixion flowered in London like a tree, and the wounds were made in Cambridge, red as oleanders.

"Remember this, at the ringing of the three bells."

Back at Madame Gongora's, I find that the sun has risen and is shining in the window on my typewriter. I sit down and begin to write.

I start with the first thing that jumps into my head. It is the day before I am supposed to go to Strasbourg, for Christmas. I am standing in front of the fireplace, Aunt Melissa is telling me the name of the place I am supposed to go to, the place where I should take a room, a students' rooming house, apparently somewhere near the university or the Botanical Gardens or something. She reads off the paper the name of the street: "Rue de l'Observatoire," and I, who am paying not enough attention, or maybe am embarrassed about something, say:

"What's that? Rue de l'Abattoir?"

She was surprised, and a little offended, I think. The whole thing immediately became immensely complicated. Nothing more was said but just that. I think she tried to make some kind of a joke about "What kind of a neighborhood do you think we want you to take rooms in, anyway?" I myself was not shocked at the idea of living near the slaughterhouse, because I lived near the slaughterhouse once, in a French village, and never heard any cries of animals or smelled the smell of slaying, and didn't think twice about it.

I have never forgotten that. Nor have I forgotten how complicated the whole thing continued to be, because in Strasbourg I was supposed to meet her friend the professor, who, I was told, would have a red beard and would carry, according to his own declaration, "une canne à tête de chien." No doubt he would hold up the carved handle of his cane at people getting off the train until somebody recognized the signal: that would be me.

And I, with my copies of Plato's *Apologia* (Loeb Classics) and Goethe's *Tasso* in my bag, I stand on the Strasbourg station and nulla canna hundshandel, nossir, niente, nientissimo. No rousse barbe, no. Wo ist der Herr Professor? Ist nicht gelangen! The herr no vinu: I see no canes, let alone dog-headed, let alone held in evidence by a man with a broad black hat and a red beard. This is a pretty picture in the imagination which, in fact, never gets realized in my experience.

I take out my little piece of paper covered with instructions. Rue de l'Abattoir is crossed out, naturally, for Rue de l'Observatoire, and whatever number it was. Then, there is the name of the professor: Professor H. There is another name, which I can't quite connect up with all the others, but it is "Cercle Evangélique." I assume that must have something to do with Professor H. and the Rue de l'Observatoire.

Clatsch, Clatsch. We go racing along the walled river in the gray of winter, in a trolley full of Alsatians talking in German. I am shocked. (Today some German is probably riding the same trolley, horrified to hear them all talking French.) We come to a section that I have seen in a million postcards, with large and small buildings, all something vaguely like the Reichstag, only the postcards didn't say Strasbourg, but Bremen, Magdeburg, Frankfurt am Main, Emden, Leipzig, Hannover, Erfurt, Koenigsberg, Berlin. South Kensington was never as heavy as this! Cannons, equestrian statues, and the libraries look out between the trees like bear traps or Bismarck.

Rue de l'Observatoire. All the way down I think of the abattoirs that surround me on all sides. The façades of the buildings are carved with big stone kidneys, livers, and clavicles and all the intimate details of life in the slaughter-house. The goddess Minerva stands among steam engines with her big trap closed and her spear in the face of everything that was ever any good. Her steel shield overshadows the world. The half light is cold and feels like snow. The day exhales a faint, gemuetlich smell of disinfectant and stale cigars. I come to the number on my paper and ring the bell.

I stand in the doorway, overhung by all kinds of heavy pediments of stone. Willkommen. Finally a window opens somewhere above me. I look up at the woman, white-haired, red-faced, rather fierce.

"Der Herr Professor H., ist er jetzt zu Hause?"

Never heard of him. Who? Der *Herr?*

I mention names. Aunt Melissa.

Never heard of her, either.

No reason why she should have. Just thought I would try it. Carefully my dry lips try to make some more German.

"Diese Frau hatte mir gesagt dasz ich hier ein Wohn-zimmer bekommen könnte: enfin, elle m'avait recommandé votre "

"This is a house for female university students only."

Instantly I am aware of the tall, short, fat, skinny, blond, wispy, irritable, shortsighted, pale, sentimental, ugly virgins that live in this house.

"Et alors, Monsieur le Professeur H. n'habite pas ici, chez vous?"

The word Nein rings like a big brass bell on the thin air of winter.

You would be extremely kind, Gnädige Frau, if you would explain to me whether or not this is the Cercle Evangélique, which is where Professor H. lives. If this isn't it, where, then, can it be found?

This much she knows: she replies at once:

"Finkmattstrasse, Acht."

"Huit, Rue Finkmatt? Merci, madame!"

Willkommen und Abschied! I got out of there in a hurry. Why mincen de worde? Cur necesario plus verbio? Niet! Me mit meine maleta scrambling after de trolleiwagen, el tranvía, rattling and clattering back to the older sections.

Thus they continue, les voyages. A half-formed character

in the bilingual mazes of this antique capital interessantis-
sime, curios, tudesque, until the monuments of all the un-
happiest instants of the nineteenth century give place to
less grandeur, and the vision can wander where it pleases,
with comparatively little offense.

Suffice it to say that our traveler, bringing to a swift
completion his round trip from one side of the city to the
other, returns to within a stone's throw of the Bahnhof,
enters the spick and span evangelical doors of a protestant
student hostel at 8, Finkmattstrasse, where he finally finds
Professor H. in a red beard and a light jacket for reading,
with the canne à tête de chien in his closet. He is admiring
the works of William Blake, Jakob Boehme, Gautama
Buddha, Karl Barth, and many others too numerous to mention.

Such are the complications that disentangle themselves
from any train of thought beginning with the time Aunt
Melissa stood in front of the fireplace, in the London flat, and
told me where to look for a room in Strasbourg.

Siga, hombre, escriba lo que piensa! Other occasions!

It is my eighteenth birthday. There is a little sun. I ride
back in the bus from Dulwich, where Uncle Rafe sent me
to see a man who would tell me where to find rooms in
Italy, where to live for very little in Rome, would tell me
who to see, would give me letters of introduction. My
pockets are full of careful information in his handwriting,
and of letters. In my pocket, also, are my passport, my
tickets, and the letters from Uncle Rafe to people in the
South of France.

Whenever I went in the high-roofed taxis to get the boat
train at Victoria, I went with letters in my pockets and
ideas, given me by Uncle Rafe and his friends.

Look, I still carry, eight years afterwards, the wallet Uncle

Rafe gave me for a present. It was the best wallet I ever saw, from Finlay's, in Bond Street.

On my eighteenth birthday, this wallet is new, and smells fine, and is full of tickets to Italy.

The evening of the day I am eighteen, we have dinner at the Café Royal, wc scc a film, we go to the Café Anglais, maybe we have some champagne. I have never forgotten it.

The next day, I take the boat train.

In Uncle Rafe's flat I did not have to pretend to admire the things I thought were ridiculous, and did not have to pretend to disparage the things I admired.

When I walked with him in the street, I did not have to make respectful double-talk about horses, or the Prince of Wales, or good sound red-faced girls as grim as cabbage, or Church of England parsons, or British woolens, or mixed hockey, or the Prime Minister, or quaint cockney humor, or motorcars, or golf.

There was no necessity to pretend to be in favor of Bournemouth or Weston super Mare. I was not obliged to pay reverence to St. Pancras Station, or the late Queen, or Georgian poets, or Rudyard Kipling, or the *Morning Post.* It was not essential to believe that, without the presence of the sensible English, India would fall to pieces and all the ignorant natives would simply die.

I did not have to conceal my belief that Picasso and Matisse and Cézanne were not crazy, were not trying to fool the suspicious millionaires, but were good artists. I did not have to pretend Blake was less of a poet than Matthew Arnold or that I liked Browning one bit.

Supposing I made a list of the things that I heard of, first of all, from Uncle Rafe? It would be very long.

It would be made up of the names of books, of painters, of cities, of kinds of wine, of curious facts about all the people in the world, about races and about languages and about writing. Only from my father did I learn what would

make a longer list than that of the things I first heard of
from Uncle Rafe.

From him I first heard of Evelyn Waugh, of Céline's
Journey to the End of the Night, of the picture galleries in
the Rue de La Boétie, in Paris, of the paintings of Chagall,
the films of René Clair, the films the Russians once made
that were good; of Joyce, of Scriabin's *Poème de l'extase,*
of flamenco music, of the kind of country Spain was; of all
these things, some were important, some were merely curious, like the story of D. H. Lawrence being sick all over the
table, at the banquet given for him at the Café Royal.

But from my father I had already heard of Blake, and
Cézanne, and Picasso, and Gregorian music, and Dante,
and the legends of saints, and the story of St. Peter's denial
of Christ: all of these were things of a different kind of
importance.

One evening we are having supper in the Monseigneur,
to hear Douglas Byng. The place is garish and stupid,
and the large table next to us fills with people who do
not look especially awkward to me, but Uncle Rafe says:

"They are in town from the suburbs, and in a minute
they will all order consommé madrilène. People from the
suburbs always order consommé madrilène as soon as they
see it on the menu."

Immediately, from amid the murmur of voices, I can
hear the words, "Consommé madrilène," spoken with a little
complacency. I am filled with astonishment and admiration.

Five years later I hang on a strap in the Seventh Avenue
subway in New York, swinging from side to side in the
yellow-lighted, crowded heat, and before my eyes is a white
card and a picture of red, jellied soup, and the sign says:

"White Rose jellied consomme madrilene."

I am still amazed at Uncle Rafe's knowledge of the world.

The last time I left London. I have come down from Cambridge the day of a royal wedding: Prince George will

marry the Princess Marina of Greece, who, everybody says, is attractive. London is crowded. The train from Cambridge was full of people from the country, carrying baskets of food. Along Piccadilly, already, people are lining up, early in the morning, most of them sitting on camp stools.

Sad, drab singers playing accordions and walking with accomplices who hold a cap out, work their way along the silent crowd. Bunting stirs in the wind: it seems to be going to rain. The pavement is beginning to be lined, without a break for miles, by hundreds of women in dark coats and shapeless hats and untidy hair, hundreds of men in tweed coats and flannels, with their hats on too straight, smoking pipes; men in caps, with stringy little scarves around their necks, men like bantamweight boxers, standing hunched up with their hands in their pockets and Woodbines stuck to their lips.

Upstairs, later on, the windows of the buildings will be thrown open, and the upper and upper middle classes will take their places in chairs in the windows, and look down upon the heads of the dark, impassive crowd underneath them, where the men and women have now begun to peer into crude, small homemade periscopes made of cardboard and hand mirrors and a little glue.

I have been caught in the crowd, and lost, and made my way out of it again, and come north as far as Oxford Circus.

Some children come along the street with little blue and white flags. I wonder if there is anything in the papers today recalling the heroic death of Byron at Missolonghi.

And maybe the other reason I have Byron on my mind is that the telephone number where I must reach Elaine, now, at Harrow is Byron something or other.

I have no time left, this last morning, to finally say good-by to anybody, except by phone. Some people I have at least called on during the week: "Well, I am leaving. Yes, for good." And so on.

Three days ago I more or less said good-by at lunch, at Uncle Rafe's flat. But I had promised not to leave without stopping in again on my last day. Now it is the last day, and I am not going to call on anybody, because I haven't time left any more.

There are some friends of mine from Cambridge waiting in a pub near Oxford Circus with their sad jokes about the royal wedding, about drunkenness, about Cambridge.

We stand around like little Byrons, and I am ashamed.

Hooray for Greece.

Somebody lets off a champagne cork in the back, and there is some cheering.

I don't know what I am saying any more; I don't know what I believe. Everybody that asks me a question gets a different answer.

"Really, old man, where are you going?"

"To be a planter in the West Indies."

"What will you plant?"

"Novels and dramas; tragicomedies, within the creaking sound of the windmills on a hill in Barbados."

"Have you ever written anything, except in the Granta?"

"No, I wouldn't know how. But now I will begin to learn in the green uplands of Venezuela."

Vive la happy Grece, dont les diplomatichi machinacaos haben por fin sus frutis! Matrimonios, hip! Prinzessa, hop! Hola, felix couple! The brides wear gowns as big as churches. The Prinz is all covered with medals, so bright. His mustache is most romantic. Unter dien bearskins, sieht man der Schnurrbart glänzen, like Goethe saw the orange blossoms in the Laubs of funny Italien.

They say they will be married in several dozen ceremonies: the Greek, the Christian English, the civil, and finally, to please the lower classes, the Methodist, which is not so distinct from the civil, but then, noblesse oblige. Think of the Greek Archbishop with his beaver and his complicated hats.

Think of the sallow, kindly Anglican prelates, or is it pri-
mates? How they flute out like frail old woodwinds the
words:

"Do thou, George, etc., etc., take this woman . . . ?"

I always say the English marrage cirrimony is so luftly.

"Really old man, jokes apart, and all that rot, what are
you going to do in America?"

"Instantly get a job on several newspapers in the city of
New Orleans, romantic New Orleans, or maybe just prosaic
New York."

"Oh, I say now, old chap, is that what you really mean?"

"Perhaps I will go to Nevada and become the owner of a
mine. Perhaps, on the other hand, I will attend the New
School for Social Research, and develop a sense of responsi-
bility, a sense of duty."

"Duty to what?"

"Oh, anything. Facts. Graphs. Propaganda analysis. Propaganda writing. Something or other. Take a course in who's
planning to murder Trotsky in his Mexican villa six years
from now. Something like that. It doesn't make a great deal
of difference, just so long as you feel earnest enough about
it."

Los paisanos gritan, vive the Greeks! Up the Creeks! Hup!
Hup! Hurroo! Cocoriquen como gallos! Champagni, mis-
erables! Ça coute cher, quand même. But, we shout also:

"For us too: come on: champagne. The old chap's going
off to America. Come on, what do you say, after all!"

That was when I took a handful of change and went
upstairs to the lounge, where the telephone stood all open,
unprotected from the tables full of conversation.

I made a list of the numbers on a piece of paper. Elaine,
the Frobishers (who happened to be in London), one or
two others, and finally Uncle Rafe.

That is the one I call first.

I put the coin in the box and dial the number, and the

words are already in my mind. "Rushing through London. Afraid I must apologize for saying good-by this way, finally. Apologize for everything else, too. Sorry about Cambridge. Good-by."

Aunt Melissa will answer.

I wait for the ringing to stop.

Then "Hello." I try to say it all very fast and hang up before she realizes I am drunk. I forget what I have said, but it is all over. She obviously knows I'm drunk, and I am leaving without saying good-by.

I had learned in the novels that questions of right and wrong didn't exist. I had learned from the laughter of the English in the corners of bars and from the presence of so many whores in London that pleasure was what was applauded. I had learned from somewhere, maybe from the parsons, that it was all right to have a good time so long as you didn't interfere with the good time of anybody else.

Now I found out that, in practice, I was not able to realize how much my pleasures might hurt somebody else until too late.

But I didn't know how to say so, because problems of right and wrong didn't exist, as everybody knew. We were merely put on earth to enjoy ourselves without hurting anybody else.

When it came time for them to take away my scholarship at Cambridge, and when it came time for me to go away from England for good, I wanted to say I was wrong, but didn't know how, because the word wrong didn't exist, no, not in the novels.

When it came time for me to say good-by, and say I was sorry because I had lost my scholarship at Cambridge (which included being sorry for a year that would make the saddest novel you ever heard of), I could not say it, because I hadn't any words to say it with. I wanted to say I was sorry, but the word sorry is the one you use when you step on some-one's foot, in the bus. I wanted to confess that I had done wrong, but confession is ill bred, and embarrassing for every-one concerned in it, the one who makes and the one who has to hear the confession. I wanted to say I had sinned, but there was no such thing as sin: sin was a morbid concept, and if you had it in your mind, this concept, it would poison you entirely and you would go crazy.

But what most of all had struck me dumb were the two questions that I even feared to ask myself: If I am here to have a good time without hurting other people, why is it, first, that you can't have the pleasures everybody believes in without hurting somebody? And why is it, second, that you never get the pleasure you expect anyway?

So, I had nothing to say, and sat like a man ready to be shot.

I may add that I composed, and then tore up, the follow-ing telegram. Since I did not send it then, I send it now. It comes as the conclusion of this, my chapter.

TELEGRAMA 1934. ADDIU INGLATERRA, MALHEUROIS ME VEO, MARCHANDOME POR LA MER HASTA LO LONTANU. SI FECI MALUM, ONCLE, ME RIPIENTO, PERO NO SE SABE COMO. PURQOI NO COMPRENNI KE SE APLAUDEN TANTO LES PLAISIRS EN LOS ROMANS, MIENTRAS EN LA VITA VIENEN CONDANNAT. DORENAVANT EN AMERIK FACCIO LO SERIOUSSE. PERHAPS. CONFUSUS, NO LONGER COMPREHENDO NADA, CHERS AMIGOS. BYRON AND SHELLEY, WHOM I HATE, ME CONFRONTAN CON SUS NERVOSI FIGURE ROMANTIK. JE CLAME, EMBARRASSAT, PURKI NO SOIS HEUREUIS, EH? HELAS, NO SE SABE. ADELANTE, POBRE JOVEN. PRIERE DE PARDONI EL INGRATITUD. ADDIU, INGLATERRA, ADDIU—PER-DON—MERCI.

XVI

It is the middle of the afternoon. The summer has disappeared: I walk along a street that looks like winter and smells like the sweet thick mists of winter.

I walk along this London street, going home to the house I live in, in the false June. Here the street has filled with a quiet mist that smells like all the suburbs of London, all the provincial cities of England.

I walk in the midst of the tea-smelling mists, among all the rows of houses in England. I walk among all the brick walls and windows and aspidistras of England, and the sick air smells sweet as a brewery. I look across all the roofs of England, before I knew there was a war. I see the thousands of chimneys in rows, whose smokes lean one way into the mist: in all the houses of England they are boiling tea and potatoes. But not much else.

This street is a general statement of many things that I remember as sad.

The smoke of Players' cigarettes is thin and sweet in the third-class carriages of the L.M.S., like going and coming from school. I remember all the brickyards of England that went by the windows of my train when I went back to school.

Walking in this street is as quiet as walking on the platforms of all the stations in England without expectancy of ever getting anywhere, except to another station made out of the same bricks, covered with the same signs.

The electric lights are on in the houses I remember, and they are finishing tea, in January 1932.

Everybody pushes back his chair from the dining-room table of the house in Sheffield. The parents of my friend from school listen to what I say. ("My father," said my friend, "says he would be interested if you could explain to him a poem by Ezra Pound.")

The father is fat and smiles all over his red face and sits, alert, with his hands planted on his knees. Alert. Smiles.

I talk. My finger points at the lines in the book, my book.

The maid goes in and out of the room.

His mother is contented because his father is alert over something. Sharp man! Doesn't see anything in this modern poetry, but willing to be ·persuaded. Demonstration!

The maid crumbs the table. The room smells of herrings that we had for tea. It smells of bread.

"Then, if I understand you, this poem is about a girl?" Sharp. He smiles, superpolite about the poetry.

"Yes, you see."

Sirs, when you take off your cuffs to eat fish, do not slip them back on to talk about the poets. Sirs, if you were really interested in books, you would talk about them the same way you talk about golf and dart games. Sirs, if you dress up in a particular suit to listen to poetry in, then you do not like poetry. Sirs, who likes poetry will like it in his shirt as well as in his suit and hat. Sirs, if you inquire about poetry believing it to be something that is loved, like yachts, by the rich, then you hate poetry as much as the rich themselves.

"Well," he says, "I am ready and willing to admit that, in part, this poem is meaningful. However, for myself, I prefer the Operas of Alice Oats, or the slicky slick cantatas of Constable Hubbard-Hoof."

Outside, in the darkness of January 1932, the tramcars lean down the hill into Sheffield. Below us the world is full of confusion of lights, and the whole city is cold and smells of bread.

Out there is a huge mystery of people who eat margarine and potatoes and believe in the Sheffield Wednesday. The tramcars move back and forth. They cross among the dark mountains of slag.

We step down into the street, in the darkness of January 1932. The air is like cold water full of melted sugar. I shiver in my coat, amazed at the parades of posters in the semi-darkness advertising beer, jam, and tobacco. The pale windows of the sweetshops and tobacconists echo to the iron cries of children, and the gaslights in the rows of houses shine green in every window.

We come to a theater near the dark center of the city, which bristles with the towers of guildhalls and the top-heavy cornices of black hotels.

Inside the theater we sit on benches next to the iron columns of the balcony.

Actors, with the footlights shining brightly on their chins and cheeks, throw their voices high up into the roof of the theater, and gaze after the trajectory of their voices through the eye shadow around their eyes.

Laughter, very lonely, answers them suddenly from the four people in the gallery, for the play is *Charley's Aunt*.

All the houses are closed in this London street. Here and there the windows are boarded over, shuttered. Here and there are sandbags, and sand buckets standing in the doorways, to be thrown when fire bombs fall and burn their chemicals on the streets and houses.

It is not really summer. The air smells like the football

fields of the Midlands, where the crowds grow back into the shadows of the stands like dark and sooty gardens full of faces. Then from everywhere rises, off the crowd, the blue mist of pipe and cigarette smoke, and the glad air fills with the breath of beer.

The cries of thousands of men in the stands at games of football sound, in the distance, sad like the sound of bagpipes; their cheering, in the distance, might be the cheering of the crew going down on a ship. Because, it is said, sometimes a ship has lifted up her bows and gone down sternward into the depths of ocean, in a naval battle, and of the sailors many never save themselves but line the decks and bridges and cheer when she sinks, as if it were glorious to go down to the bottom of the sea in a defeated cruiser.

Sometimes the cheering of the football crowds in Leicester sounds like this, and in the middle of the cheering, in 1932, already in the air was heard the noise of bombers. Everybody looked up but nothing was seen.

I am standing on the platform of a station, in December 1932, and see through the mist the tall chimneys of the factories and the crenelated breweries built to look like towers of fortified castles, and somewhere behind the rows of houses is a football field where I can hear the pathos of the distant cheering. The cheers rise and fall, and if you forget what they are for, they suddenly sound like lamentations. They make a shrill, iron discord like motors, or like sirens, but the voice is the voice of a great, sad thing: a crowd.

Then the voice dies down, and I cannot bear to see the sinking of the ship or hear the drowning of that cheer.

The train comes in destroying everything.

I turn the corner. At the end of the street is the park. On the right, the steps to the house of Madame Gongora. I look up at my window, on the second floor.

In my window stand two strangers, with their hands

folded behind their backs, looking down at me. They see that I am surprised. They do not turn away. They continue to look down at me, from the window of my own room.

They are in uniform.

"Ah, signor," says Valdes, "dos Mountzours ke vous esperent, arriba. Gendarmes without a doubt. Molto fini, curiosi. Preguntan questioni sans finir, sobre lo que vos excribo en la cliqueti-maquin fur scribo. Examine pages of vonis manuscrito with larmes de futil incomprehension. Now stretched out in les chaises cum atitudinos disgustadiz di folor y cansadez, per experar vd. Pronto! Get ready! Hombre!"

I go up the stairs and open the door of the room.

"Well," says one officer to the other, "finally!"

The first speaks.

"Are you the following person: T. J. Merton?"

The other one has a swagger stick and smacks it against his boot with an idle, moody gesture.

"I am. What have I done now?"

The officers look at one another, and back at me.

"Your papers," says the first, "if you don't mind."

He takes them in his hand. Flips open the passport and says:

"What on earth is this?"

"Passport."

"Nonsense, there's no such country as Casa: look at this, Captain, will you: 'Paseportu de Casa, Diplomaticu, officialdo.' This is sheer nonsense." He fixes me with a penetrating stare and says: "*Are you aware that Casa is a Spanish word meaning House? There is no country called House.*"

"*In my language, Casa means Home.*"

"Oh, indeed. Home. *And where did you get your passport?*"

"*Home.*"

"Do you know what I think?" said the officer. "I think you made this passport yourself, and trumped up this whole thing as a joke. However, this is no time for pleasantries, my friend. Would you mind giving us your real passport, that is, if you have a valid passport of any existing nation?"

"You will find it among the package I just gave you."

"This one?" He says, "American?"

"I suppose so."

"What do you mean, you suppose so? Look here, I warn you to stop being funny, this is no time for jokes. Either you are an American or you are not. Which is it?"

"Read the passport, then. Make up your own mind. I'm no more American than I am English. But I had to have some kind of a passport, didn't I, to show to people like you."

"You are under arrest," shouted the officer in a lowering rage.

"You can't arrest him yet," said the other coolly. "Go ahead, read his passport."

The other officer examined my American passport closely, and finally, after a long time, closed it and handed it back to me, saying:

"Here. All in order. Probably a clever fake, but I can't prove it." Turning to his companion, he said: "Native of *Casa*. Can you imagine? The Americans put him down as a native of this place he invented!"

Then he turns back to me.

"You are an American," he said emphatically. "*Do you understand? You are an American. You are not a citizen of Casa. Your passport says you are an American.*"

What he says makes me feel, suddenly, very sad, and I answer him, turning away, "Of course. I am a citizen of anything you say."

"Oh no, you are not an American just because I say it, but because you are. Dammit, you've got to have a nationality. Otherwise you won't be allowed to travel at all. As it is, I don't see who let you into England, and I think there is every reason to arrest you, and have you up for trial."

"What for?" says the other.

"As a 'native of Casa,'" sneers the first.

But the second one is smarter. He says:

"In a word, that parody passport you carry, that Casa passport, indicates a certain *attitude* on your part. A certain *cynical attitude*, am I right?"

"Not cynical, no, sir."

"It is a kind of a sneer at human institutions, I gather."

"No, I would not sneer at anything, even human institutions."

"You've got to have human institutions, you know. You can't live without laws and regulations, you know."

"Of course not, society is inescapable."

"We all admit it would be nicer if human institutions worked a little better. I hope you aren't agreeing with me just to be polite. I give you credit for more intelligence than that."

"Oh no, sir, I realize that society has a definite place and a function, sir, indubitably. Oh yes indeed."

"But there is another order, a higher order?"

I answer:

"There are two orders, the order of law and the order of freedom, and I'll give you two guesses which one I think is the more important."

"Very well, I realize that. Unfortunately we are all living under law."

"Who said so?"

"You have to eat. Self-preservation is the first law of nature."

"Yes, but ask the lilies of the field concerning the first law of nature; they toil not, neither do they spin."

"You have to live in society."

"I just rendered unto Caesar a choice of true and false passport? That is a matter for society to judge, and I will abide by the judgment. I will do what society tells me."

"That is negative."

"The things I owe Caesar can best be said negatively: that is, I owe him whatever he asks that does not conflict with what I owe on another level of loves and debts."

"You owe Caesar this much, too, to sacrifice yourself for the good of the state. You are a social animal, a creature of ethics."

"I gave you my social animal's passports. I will wear any label you hitch onto my collar, in the world's wide prison. But though you give me a license that says I am a social animal, I continue to know I am a child of God, and while you talk about your abstract ethics, which is a science, I will pray to learn, on another level that overcomes and includes all the other levels, a concrete love which is not an abstract science but a way of life, and only exists in actions. I will buy all the passports required of me by Caesar's petty clerks, but my passports do not tell anything like my real identity, nor do they have anything much to do with what I live for. I will fulfill all the conditions the laws ask me to fulfill. I will suffer the laws the state may make, and not even think about complaining of them, because there have to be laws; we are all born in sin. But when you ask me to tell my real name by means of passports, and live my life in terms of total allegiance to human systems, I can only answer you in a set of equivocal jokes, by which I am all but helpless to tell you that I don't understand what you are talking about."

"We are not asking you to give up your religion. If you believe that sort of thing, that is very nice for you. But remember you are living in the world: you have to live according to nature, protect yourself, feed yourself, reproduce yourself. But the world is competitive. If you were all alone, you would soon find out how hard the world is. You owe more than a negative allegiance to society, because through society you get everything essential to life."

"Buenos días, signior. I am a native of Casa, amigo de los lirios en el campo. Foxes have holes and birds of the air have nests, and I will lie down among the meadow flowers in Casa, where I come from, but this place is full of tree stumps and the ground is swampy and my hands are caked with the peat and I cannot rest in the bog you speak of as giving me everything essential to life."

"You have to eat, and to eat you have to work and compete with others, and in the competition you would be overwhelmed by everybody else if the state did not protect your rights."

"Hola, chico, tu sprichts verbos molto solemni, clingen clangen como lo matemático, muy sutil, ha? Lo stato mi protegatz big bags of blunderbuss, mister. Consider the birds of the air. Who feeds all things of every kind? The Society puts up big tin birdbaths in the park, but whom do the birds look to for their life's bread?"

"Themselves, my friend."

"O oiseaux excellentissimi! Up and down they go, the wise progressive birds, plowing and reaping in the fields, comprando granum, sowing the grain they bought with their savings, in the furrows of the fields. Cunado ha vd. vist lis oiseaux cultivando lou pais, hey? Di mi lou risponst, uffizir!"

"This is nothing but equivocation. You are deliberately refusing to understand my terms, but I say work is compulsory because work is liberty. (Le travail est obligatoire, car le travail c'est la liberté.)"

"When I was a child in Casa they read me the story of Elijah fed by the ravens, and the poverty of St. Francis."

"All superstitions are forbidden by the state. Who read you those legends?"

"Angels."

The first, and less informed, of the two officers, who had long been trying to contain his impatience, finally burst out:

"That is enough. Can't you see he's nothing but a trickster? He knows very well that the stuff he's saying hasn't any meaning; he doesn't even understand it himself, I wager. He's merely trying to make fun of the orderly processes of government."

"We can't arrest him for being eccentric," said the other. "And, I must say, I've rather enjoyed this little talk. Get the other person's point of view, see how silly it really is."

"Wait," said the first, "we didn't come here merely to visit this person, and have a little chat about some bit of fantasy he has in his head. There is something else."

"Yes?"

"You said this passport was not an adequate identification of yourself, that is, in your own opinion. Just what do you mean?"

"Nothing for you to worry about. There is nothing the laws can ask me that will give an answer identifying me properly. I don't consider my name and all my various license numbers of the licenses you give me to exist either define my existence or entitle me to it, and none of them describe me as I am."

"Let us review these facts," said the officer, whipping out a little notebook. "It may transpire that we know a little more about you than you think." After glancing at the other significantly, he begins.

"Name: Thomas James Merton. We've already been over that. Date of birth: January 31, 1915. 26 years old. Notice that you are of military age, but not yet in uniform. We'll discuss that some other time. Now, here:

"Place of Birth. *Place:* what do I see under the heading of place? Do I see *Casa?* No, I do not see Casa, or Plaza, or anything else.

"Place of Birth: Prades (Pyr. Or.), France.

"You see, your lies don't do you any good; we know all about you. Now, this question of citizenship. You are a citizen of Casa? There is nothing in these papers about Casa. You were, by birth, a British subject, because your father came from New Zealand. Deny that, if you can. You crossed the Atlantic in 1916 and went to America, where you lived until 1925, then returning with your father to France, where you attended school at the Lycée de Montauban. Am I correct?

"Then," he continued, "in 1928, you went to England, where you entered a preparatory school at Ripley, Surrey, remaining there for a year, after which you went to Oakham School, and to Cambridge University. Leaving Cambridge after one year, you then, in 1934, returned once again to America, entered Columbia University, where you completed your undergraduate education and did some graduate work, meanwhile also taking steps to become an American citizen. Now am I right or wrong, my fine equivocal friend; is this information correct? Does it identify you?"

"All those things are true. However, they don't identify me, except to you, and that is no identification at all."

"Have the kindness to tell me why."

"You think you can identify a man by giving his date of birth and his address, his height, his eyes' color, even his fingerprints. Such information will help you put the right tag on his body if you should run across his body somewhere full of bullets, but it doesn't say anything about the man himself. Men become objects and not persons. Now you complain because there is a war, but war is the proper state for a world in which men are a series of numbered bodies. War is the state that now perfectly fits your philosophy of life: you deserve the war for believing the things you believe. In so far as I tend to believe those same things and act according to such lies, I am part of the complex of responsibilities for the war too. But if you want to identify me, ask me not where I live, or what I like to eat, or how I comb my hair, but ask me what I think I am living for, in detail, and ask me what I think is keeping me from living fully for the thing I want to live for. Between these two answers you can determine the identity of any person. The better answer he has, the more of a person he is."

"Oh, Lord," said the officer, "now what are you talking about! If you want to find out a man's identity, ask him to tell you his favorite riddle! I want plain facts or nothing."

"When you get one, you're very likely to get the other with it."

"And anyway, supposing I asked you those metaphysical questions," said the second, and more informed, of the officers, "would your answer have any meaning?"

"My answer would be a series of concrete expressions of what you have just said abstractly."

"Then why don't you give us your answer?"

"I am all the time trying to answer both you and myself. I am all the time trying to make out the answer, as I go on living. I live out the answer to my two questions myself and the answer may not be complete, even when my life is ended: I may go on working out the answer for a long time after my death, but at last it will be resolved, and there will be no further question, for with God's mercy I shall possess not only the answer but the reality that the answer was about."

The first officer rolled his eyes in despair.

"That is what I am writing about," I added.

He seemed on the point of having a fit. Then in a totally different voice he cried:

"Ach, Herr! Signior! Vd. me faz volver girar mi moboli capitals di cerebello! Ich larmoye at de auge, Ik blutet an de nase, Ik zittert an de dentes, Ik clap clap under the ribben bonen vor intellektual hunger after der verstanden dieses ratsels! No, thanks!

"Marching is besser, verdad?

"Hand me your handkerchief, my nose bleeds for awe and misunderstanding!

"Tip me a couple of pennies, that I may go out and buy fruit; my wits are parched!

"Slap me the info in Greek. I seem to know the dead languages better.

"Come, Uffizir Charles, this dandy is hop-happy with American jests he read in the libbers of the medievals and the top-heavy texts of antique lattins of the Meddle Evo, and the Arisdoddle and Ploddos of antshinned Greece.

"Hup. Hup, Charlie, hup out of the chairs, you dog; this is where we pack up our heap of official parcels and drop our questions like a bushel of papayas. Let's retire for the evening, and I'll soak my head in the intellectual showers of a film or two! Hup, hup, Karl, heraus, Kapitan, back to the sundry barracks and report that this boy come from Casa, and as far as we're concerned the sooner he's home there and out of the way from the English hic et nunc, the better it will be for the war!"

"As for me," said the second officer coldly as they both went out the door together (the first one nursing his nosebleed), "as for me, I shall suggest deportation, if not prison. But we can't have him around here, not in a time of war."

XVII

I am on my way to France. I don't know how I am supposed to get there. I believe I am to cross the Channel with two British intelligence officers, in a torpedo boat, which will turn us over to a French fishing boat off the coast, somewhere near Deauville, or perhaps farther west.

After that, I must, somehow, get to Paris by myself. I will probably be landed somewhere alone, as the intelligence officers won't want anything to do with me, on enemy ground, nor I with them.

I try to imagine what it will be like inland in the fields a few miles from the Channel, with the dunes behind me, and cottages and apple trees to the right and to the left, and in front of me one of the big Thomas Cook signs in English, with a crude picture of the Sphinx and the words "VISIT EGYPT."

Meanwhile, I am in a partly ruined hotel in Folkestone, on top of the cliffs. The two top floors have been burned out, but on the ground floor aviators and antiaircraft gunners play the pinball machines together, in the wide, bare rooms of the ground floor, from which all furniture has been removed and replaced with benches and folding chairs and crude, temporary-looking tables.

In this hotel, it is continually winter. The wide, bleak rooms are full of the smell of salt and the chill of rain. The loud and awkward people in white flannels have been removed like the chairs and sofas and tea tables and potted palm trees. A billiard table is left, and a piano, which now an airman plays, badly, with a cigarette in his lips. He goes endlessly over the same tune, "Oh Johnny, Oh Johnny, how you can love." Each time he makes the same mistake in the same place, goes back and picks it up, and plays it through.

I look out at the sea, the Channel, a little rough in the evening light. Down below me is the jetty where the Channel steamers used to come in, where you used to get off and walk along the narrow, roofed platform, and smell the smell of England in the big, dirty refreshment room: the smell of tea, and buns, and beer.

There also you used to hear the first of English speech, the clipped, chirping insults of the barmaids and the porters (the porters in their Victorian uniforms with narrow, straight visored caps!).

Every time I ever landed at Folkestone, I learned all over again the immense difference between England and France. In England everything seemed smaller, neater, more confined. It was like coming from the outdoors into a room, but a room where everything was in place, where everything was ordered, safe, and dull. Later, I learned, there was something terrible in the room that made you want to escape.

England was full of the houses of the poor, crowded together up and down the hills in rows and red rows. France was full of long roads lined with trees. England was a park with very ornamental trees and strictly formal sheep, iron railings, gates, stiles, and hedges everywhere: everything in place. England was full of imaginary people who belonged in no world at all, only the novels of Dickens. France was more real, less of a silly dream, and had in it fewer Peggotys and Aunt Betsys. The only Ivanhoes dressed up in tweeds in France were there to be swindled by the waiters and laughed at by the witty poor: they had come from England.

I am sad to see this jetty here, because of my father, who is dead ten years.

In the spring of 1926, we walked the length of the train at Folkestone, with my father reviling England, because there was only one third-class carriage, and that was jammed with people, all along the corridors from end to end, so that you could scarcely move. All the men and old ladies stood like insolent, offended sheep. Their insolence was contagious, and their plainness and pride an insult, even to me, a child.

However, in this hotel, it is not possible to think very long of the past, or even to think of anything in particular except the war, for this is the front line.

While I was writing a moment ago, I began to hear the thunder of gunfire in the distance, and, looking out over the Channel, I saw the evening sky fill with flashes. As I look up, it begins again, and stops, and then begins again. The aviator continues to play the same monotonous tune on the piano.

The gunfire on the other side of the Channel has moved farther west and is now coming from another place. The flashes are brighter, because it is getting dark rapidly now. I suppose the flashes are the explosions of bombs.

When they grow a little louder, the piano stops playing. All the airmen and soldiers begin to walk idly toward the windows, and watch the sky, across the Channel, in silence. There are long intervals between flashes, which come two or three or more in a group. The gunfire is more or less continual now. After what seems to be quite a long time, the flashes cease altogether and the gunfire stops, and already, before the guns are silent, the air is filled with the sound of planes, very high, coming back.

Yet it isn't long since it started, at all: barely fifteen or twenty minutes.

The men listen to the sound of the returning planes. One, in tweeds, walks to the telephone then, lighting a cigarette, and I hear his voice speaking in a loud, exasperated tone. I catch the words:

"Bombed the invasion ports again . . . fairly heavily."

He is playing with the door of the booth, which now swings open, and I hear a complete sentence.

"The flashes of the bombs could be distinctly seen by all the delighted residents of a certain south coast town. Explosions of great force were heard, together with . . ." (The door swings shut. Through the glass, I see his lips moving, and the cigarette wags in his mouth as he talks. The door swings open again.) ". . . women and children cheered the returning units of the RAF, and I suppose that's all for tonight."

He listens to his phone for a while, says, "What?"

Then he says, "Yes, I suppose it was a pretty big show. Well, fairly big, or moderate. And listen, please, carefully: tell Jimmy to look in the top left-hand drawer, he knows where, and send me all the socks he can find. I'm having a terrible time for socks."

He hangs up the receiver and comes out of the booth.

He stops and says to me:

"Going to phone your story in, old man?"

"Oh no," I say, "not exactly."

Just because I have a pen, he takes me for a reporter.

"I'm not writing news," I say.

"Oh," he says, "features, eyewitness. More power to you."

"It's more that sort of thing, yes," I admit.

"American?" he asks me.

"In a way."

"I suppose you've talked with the American boys down here. We have two here, you know. I suppose you'll want to see them, especially; that is, if you're writing features for the American press."

"I can't see them right now," I say. "I am waiting for a man to take me somewhere, in a few minutes."

"Night fighter station, eh?" says the reporter. "You'll be thrilled. I was, the first time I was out there. Covered one of the King's visits. Thrilled, really. Didn't think I could be so moved. You'll like it."

"I look forward to an exciting evening," I reply.

"Perhaps I'll see you later. You could talk to the American boys then."

"Delighted," I say.

"Yes, you'll enjoy it here. Boys all toned up, these days. Lot of zest in this scrap, you know. The Air Force has put something new in the war, know what I mean?"

"Yes," I say, "it has, hasn't it? Individual combat in the air seems almost to have brought back the old days of knighthood, doesn't it?"

"Jove, it has, hasn't it! I wish I'd thought of that! You feature writers are pretty good on those fancy expressions, I must say."

"Oh, don't give it a thought, it wasn't my own," I reply, and at the moment I see one of my intelligence officers standing in the doorway. He signals to me; it seems the boat is ready.

"So long," says the reporter, "you'll be thrilled to death."

XVIII

I stand in the middle of the white road, Route Nationale, lined with plane trees. The road heads straight south, toward the sun, which is climbing as high as noon. Behind me is the Channel, the sea of blood between me and my island.

Standing in the grass and flowers of the roadside is a square, white, hundred-meter marker. Southwest: Amiens and Paris.

I am wearing a gray, double-breasted American suit, brown shoes that did not lose their shine from sea spray (I crossed in a torpedo boat, landing on a deserted part of the coast), a Homburg hat. I have with me my suitcase and my typewriter. That is the way I am, standing in the middle of the country, in the North of France.

I stand in the road, smelling the sweet smell of deserted France. I cannot see anyone else all down the long stretch of highway. I do not hear the sound of any car, or of anything at all. There is no one in the fields. I do not even see any cattle.

Even though the grass sings in the bright sun, I am afraid: I am afraid all the grass and flowers will sink, like a tide, and when I turn again, in a moment, the bright sea of living things, of flowers and wheat, will have melted back into the earth. And, when it has gone, then I will see what I fear: the skeletons of machines of war burned out, or smashed, or twisted, that are now all buried in the deep, waving vegetation.

I cannot believe that all this lightly moving wheat is not hiding the rusty metal of machines destroyed in battles a year ago.

I walk a little way in the warm sun. The silence scares me, too. Any minute I expect to hear guns behind me, along the coast. I expect the sky to fill up, on all sides, with the huge roar of bombers going over in a fleet so high they can hardly be seen. Yet nothing happens. In my clean, pressed American suit, I walk along this road. The trees are awake, and branches swing happily over my head.

Somewhere behind me I know what the coast looks like, still misty. I have not been near any towns. I imagine the estuary at Étaples, the pale blue, misty streets, the drawbridge destroyed by bombs, German soldiers walking out of the roofless houses.

Most days, I find, are quiet as this. They are as quiet as the days that used to come in movie comedies, when the comedians Charlie Chaplin, Laurel and Hardy, or whoever it was would be discovered still living in a trench, contentedly, amid a big pile of empty food cans, not realizing the war was over months ago. I feel like one of those comedians, walking in the middle of France under some fantastic misapprehension, all alone. The whole world has stopped doing what I imagine, by all accounts, it should be doing still, and has picked up and gone off to do something else, in some other place.

Then, at last, I am startled by some movement.

A big metal flag, standing on a structure, up out of the grass two hundred yards away, suddenly changes its position, and tilts upward with a sound that barely reaches my ear, and then remains still.

It is a railway signal. There must be tracks there, a railway line. Then I notice telegraph poles. The railroad line runs southward, parallel with the road on which I now walk slowly. I was scared by this sudden coming to life of something in the landscape. Now my apprehensive mind runs back along the line, to the signal box, where some German has just thrown the switch and changed the signal.

Some train will be coming through, soon. I wonder if it will slow down, anywhere near the signal, or stop so that I can get on. Not much chance. And anyway, for ten, then fifteen, then twenty minutes, nothing happens.

Then I hear something behind me. At first I think it is a plane, far away, in the air, then I realize it is something on the road, and I turn and see it is a truck, coming up the road quite fast. It is like no truck I ever saw before.

I do not look around, but walk straight on, lugging my suitcase and typewriter, and the truck comes closer and closer behind me, and finally I notice it is beginning to slow down.

It passes me and stops.

The German soldiers all look back at me and wait for me to come up. One of them, fluttering with his fingers the pages of a little book, looks up and cries out:

"Monter!"

They help me up.

The truck starts. I stand among the soldiers, who, with folded arms, and hands in pockets, act in no way as if they have arrested me. I realize I am getting a ride. The five soldiers in the back of the truck are small, and sallow, and look like discontented waiters from cheap restaurants in New York and Philadelphia dressed up in German uniforms. One of them, however, wears steel-rimmed spectacles. They are all taciturn, sad, and rather old. The one with the steel-rimmed spectacles keeps scowling shyly into a little book, which I see, now, is a book of French phrases. I realize that presently he is going to speak. I can see him trying to frame a sentence. I wonder what it will be.

Finally it gets out:

"Je suis musicien," is the thing he wants to say. "Je jouer le tambour." He ceases to speak, and a great sad blush begins to come over his face, and he glances at me through his glasses, and turns away his head, mortified. His elderly comrades do not seem to pay any attention to him at all.

I reply solemnly:

"Très bien! Vous êtes musicien. J'en suis très content."

There is a silence. He knows another sentence, which he does not have to look up in the book.

"Nous ne sommes pas tristes," he says very carefully. "Nous sommes très heureux."

"O, bien entendu, vous êtes très heureux, oui! Ah, par exemple! You don't have to tell me! I can see you are the happiest people in the universe. My congratulations!"

I make no attempt at any kind of a false friendly smile.

There is a silence. The soldier glances in the book. He says sourly:

"Pour nous, la vie est un rêve. Nous serons toujours jeunes."

One of the soldiers, whose cropped hair is as gray as metal, coughs sharply, continuously, for about a minute, and then stops exhausted. Yes, life is a dream! They are forever young.

"Ah, oui," I reply when the coughing has subsided, "votre èternelle jeunesse vient de votre gaité insouciante et enfantine, et la vigueur printanière de vos cinquante ans se manifeste par un fou-rire perpetuel."

The soldier listens intently to what I have just said, and then nods and says:

"Vous tenez raison."

The shadows of trees fly over the truck. I look out over the fields and see two German soldiers running a tractor. We leave them far behind. The sound of the tractor is lost. We are coming to a village.

The soldier with the little book of words says:

"Le tambour est un instrument de musique sublime."

"I do not question it for a moment," I reply.

"You are perpetually happy, with your music. You are inebriated with creativity! You are almost out of your mind!"

We fly through the village. About two kilometers outside the village he adds:

"I am always happy because I am not old."

The sign by the road is like all the blue and yellow Citroën signs I remember from my childhood, and it says Abbeville, fifteen kilometers. Maybe from there I can get a train to Paris.

The German soldiers let me off their truck in the middle of Abbeville, which is like a landscape in the moon. I am in a labyrinth of walls, with wide, cleared spaces in between and, here and there, a complete building. I see the spire of a church, through a stage set of bombed houses. In the middle of a block of spick-and-span ruins stands a hotel, intact, as if nothing had happened since 1560. Some German soldiers are sitting at tables, in front of it, under an awning, looking at the empty street.

They are like children playing house. There is nothing on the tables. But they are sitting there, I suppose, to enjoy the shade of the awning.

However, at every corner there are elaborate signposts, bristling with old and new signs, in both French and German. The signs name all the things a town should have: Bahnhof, Postamt, and so on, but you do not see these things: only a labyrinth of walls of varying height, pierced, here and there, by useless, abstract-looking windows.

And then I turn a corner, and all that I have seen turns into a dream: I am once again in a real street, lined with small, clean houses, with blue and gray wooden shutters and slate roofs. There are flowerpots in some of the windows, with flowers, red and white.

In another window farther down, a German soldier, a very old man, leans, smoking a cigar and blinking at the street, in his undershirt.

I hesitate, on this corner, and finally turn back and put down my luggage under the awning of the hotel, walk into the café, where a lady in a black dress sits behind the counter, in the big empty room, with her hands folded, and as still as a statue.

I realize she is listening to the radio, through the loud-speaker of which now comes the "Beer Barrel Polka," sung in German and frequently interrupted by the coughing of static.

All around her, the walls are covered with the old familiar signs: Amer Picon, Pernod, Dubonnet, Cassis. There is a big red Byrrh calendar, which has not been changed since August 19, 1940, nearly a year ago.

I ask for the railway timetables. Without a word, the lady points sternly to the rack, on the other side of the room. The railway timetable is, also, a year out of date.

Before I discover that, a voice begins to talk on the radio:

"Caro Populi inferior:

"Ben mas favorable beginnen unser speeches mit dem Puppels conquist, pueblos massacrat, humilissimo, abajo; nous vous tendrement lieben, pero nous vous sehr streng (suddenly) beat up, mes pauvres amis! That goes to show the moral lesson from the survival of the victuals, or should I say the revival of the biggest?

"Franzos, massacrat, humilie toi. D'ailleurs, on t'admire, cannaille. No forgetting, pobrecit, nuestro formidabili conquistu, y te tais! Give us your scraps of bread, humble brother, because our soldaten kommen at youse last May a year ago up out of the spring flowers, mighty fast, before you was aware. Give us your scraps of bread and your dregs of wine, give us your Picasso pictures and your Third Empire furniture, as if we knew the difference. Conquisti: we are the most well-bred and humane of Caesars, we smokken de cigarre, we likken de cigarretten, huffen te puffen de gud burgerliken meerschaum pipe, scrape our clean heads every once in a while with our manicured nails, jouer le violon, singen de Wagner, muy religios, besides, because our army is a perpetual Sunday school.

"But nu meminisse, Franzos conquisti, los circunstancios di su late-recent massacri from pleasant memory.

"Our humane boys come raging up out of the ground like country gods with flowers all over their hats, and the flammenwerfers all concealed in delicate blooms. Oh, wasn't we a lovely bevy of tanks, tan bellos como praticos, to come busting out of the elaborate cages of trees which our Furrier themself planned, in his garden house imagination?

"Let's look at the record, then, boys: and here is how we standen. Maginot Linie: gross metallico concreti, inquassato, horribili.

"The whole earth murmurs with machinery deep in the tunnels. Hills come to life. Huge silent mushrooms of cement come up out of the ground and point here and point there de kanonen: schreck! scrack! The silent mushroom sinks back into the earth. Underneath the tons of loam the trains of your soldiers go ringing along the military railways, transportat desde alla hasta aquí in the crinkling of an augenblick. Die Ganze Erde iss full from elevators, telephonen, hospitalization plans, free insurance, sewage disposal, collective bargaining, procès verbaux, dental clinics, y todos los milagros de la tecnología moderna. That's what *you* think!

"Alors: Nous. Tanken, Schlafwagen, Flammenwerfer, Glockenspiel, Abort, Stuka, everything besser. Besser Glockenspiels, more horrible tanks, big rubber boats, not to mention a monopoly on Tom Swift's electric rifle.

"Oh yes, gentlemen: our leader, Alfred Hitler, I think, has proved himself a jump or two ahead of you French gentlemen. The romantics, or should I say the romantically inclined, among you, seem to believe that our leader, Alfred Hitler, borrowed the notion of the flammenwerfer from that ancient German concept of Fafnir the dragon. You think so? You are entitled to think so. Have your delicious thoughts.

"But allow me to utter a discrete hatful of German breath in warning to you French gentlemen: I advise you, with an outburst of particularly heavy and inept and irritating sarcasm fretting in every pore of my big, red, gleaming, sweaty body, that our Furrier, Alfred Hitler, quite definitely meant business, and means it still as our dastardly Russian allies are finding out this minute. So put down those spoons with which you intend to menace us, and meditate a while on what happened to you who think you are so famous, so well known, and so heard of throughout the world. Resign yourselves to the fact that you are Alfred Hitler's long lost little brother, Edgar. Believe me, my French friends, you scarcely realize that for our Fewer to show sutch gnadigkeit, sudge bonhomie in his puffy, mustached countenance toward youse, is some favor for an Aryan to demonstrate toward the bunch of Jews that youse happen to be.

"Now to return to the cursus belli, and to your singularly insulting defeat, O unhappy Franzosen, which we now temper with all kinds of proffers of kindness (because of course, from the first, nobody meant anything but the sheerest, mildest, and most affectionate form of kindness).

"Krieg. Stark positiv: Krieg. We sitzen in the Sigsfreed Line with our feelings hurt to the point of intense agony, for one whole winter. German feelings smart like sunburn. Oh, wow! Insufferable! The generals scream and beat their heads against the walls of forts, in an attempt to restrain their delicate feelings. O noble rage tudesque! Hundreds of infantry sergeants weep like bulls, they are so offended at the injustice of the whole world. German feeling rises quick as the mercury in a big, inaccurate thermometer. Even the little children cannot stand the insults to the nation: they take their dolls by the foots and crash them against the side of the house. German honor begins to rage like a big out-of-date locomotive. It is too late. Feeling is too high. Teach the world a lesson.

"German honor explodes, everything goes black. Too bad for youse, you flippant, artistic Franzosen: now every German soldier is turned into a merciless Arminius with firecrackers going off continuously in every part of his head, with drums and rattles clattering in his chest, with his big lungs heaving like bellows in a forge, his arms moving like the sails of mills, his teeth hopping about like the keys of mechanical pianos and his eyes flashing like electric signs. This is the terrible moment for the whole world: every German's skull is a big wide hall full of Wagner, every German's chest is a cave full of drums, every German's breath hisses like the fuse of an explosive charge. This is the glorious moment. Somebody blows a whistle. A million unbelievable Siegfrieds, all exactly alike, rush head first at the enemy, from every possible direction, like madmen, like football players, like drunks.

"In every part of Belgium, Holland, and Northern France, the early morning air fills with clouds of parachutes, floating down as silently and gently as Portuguese men-of-war in the warm shallow water of a Florida beach.

"Hanging under every parachute is a Siegfried, holding in his hand a small, framed portrait of Hitler, reciting with tears in his eyes the German irregular verbs, or the multiplication tables.

"Shrapnel flowers all over the rivers and canals like a garden of white flowers that instantaneously disappear. The sides of the houses fall down, and tanks come rushing out into the open, shooting in more than one direction.

"Teams of Siegfrieds, like tumblers, leap instantly upon one another's shoulders at the edges of the concrete fortresses before the men inside have had time to drop their novels, and the acrobat on the top has in one hand a flame thrower and in the other a small swastika flag.

"The war is already over before it has begun. The German army is everywhere.

"Pour makken a longue story raccourci, nous voulons vous regaler with the exquisite pleasure of some interesting testimonials which we have received from all quarters in conquered countries testifying to the enthusiastic admiration of the conquered for us, their conquerors, and, incidentally, throwing some light upon our truly remarkable and never-before-seen military tactics whose swiftness and deadly efficacy surprised everyone but our Fuehrer, Arthur Hitler, who doubtless foreknows and foresees everything. First testimonial letter: A gent in the infantry (Franzos).

"'Cher Fuehrer:

"'I thinks youse is vraiment remarquable. On the morning of May —, 1940, I was working the vacuum cleaner in Blockhouse 864 outside of Sedan when I heard somebody monkeying with the general's icebox. Très peu méfiant, d'ordinaire, I must have sensed some new événement. In any case, poking my head around the door, what was my surprise to see the blockhouse was full of Germans, some with their helmets on, some with their helmets off, sitting in the easy chairs, reading the newspapers, eating the officers' cold chicken, drinking the wine, using the tooth-picks, combs, hair oil, talcum powder, and taking pictures of the whole proceedings with expensive Leica cameras. Thus I knew that the conquest of France had taken place. I turned off the vacuum cleaner, changed into civilian clothes, and made off at once without any further ado.'

"Second testimonial: Same infantries: Offizier.

"'Dear Sirs:

"'I have no doubt the textbooks of history will be at a loss to describe your interesting invasion of the —th inst. A few days ago, taking advantage of the early sun, I had set up my easel within a half mile of Blockhouse x561, in the Metz sector, and had begun to sketch, when I noticed several dozen joueurs de football (association) approaching, vetus de caleçons bleu-blanc-rouges, and carrying with them their football. Their captain asked me, politely enough, if it would inconvenience me to have them indulge in une petite partie de foot' in the midst of the landscape I was sketching, and only after I had replied that it was no inconvenience at all (thinking of perhaps enlivening the landscape with the figures of ces sportifs) did I realize that the man had ad-dressed me in German. I leaped to my feet and began to dismantle my easel, but it was too late: with a loud shout, the men in football suits had rushed upon the nearest block-house, and with the football (which contained a charge of an unbelievably powerful explosive) demolished the entire blockhouse before my very eyes. I slipped away while they were posing for the cameras of the cinemas and escaped to Marseille, where I now eke out a precarious living selling postcards.'"

"Third Testimonial letter: capitaine d'artillerie belge . . ."

But while the voice on the radio goes on, I get up again and go outside the café under the awning, where the tables are still occupied by German soldiers, but, now, probably all different individuals, although they all look exactly like the ones who were there before.

I take up my suitcase and glance around me, hesitating, looking for the sign I saw a moment before saying Bahnhof, and while I hesitate, one of the soldiers approaches me and stands sadly by, for a moment. He has something to say.

What will it be? He is a musician? He is very happy? The German Army is everlastlingly young? What is it now?

As soon as I glance at him, he steps forward and takes the suitcase and typewriter from me, straightens up, and says:

"Alles fertig, Herr Korrespondent!"

Still not quite sure whether I am being arrested, I say something brusque, the first thing that comes into my head:

"Wo gehen wir hin?"

I get an immediate answer:

"The car is waiting around the corner, in the shade; if you don't mind walking that far."

"Very good."

"Bitte schoen."

I let him precede me; we goose-step smartly away from the terrace of the café, and around the corner, to a big Mercedes-Benz, open. I get in.

"Anything else, sir?" says the soldier.

I give him some money and say:

"You have been very prompt."

Then the soldier begins to grin.

"You can thank the captain for that," he says. "He was very sore when he found out you were wandering around, alone, out there in the country."

"Well," I roared suddenly, as if I were very angry, "it was his fault, wasn't it?"

"Yes, sir," says the soldier in confusion. Then we exchange

salutes, and the driver comes running out of the hotel like a hare, looking at me wildly and pulling on his gloves.

"Back to Paris," I cry. "Nach Paris! At once, as fast as you can go."

And we leave the ruins of Abbeville in a cloud of dust.

XIX

JOURNAL: PARIS

I am alone in the street. I am looking at a big dark building, which is built in the shape of a crescent, at a corner of the boulevard. They have still not removed the sandbags from around the doors and the bases of the columns of the official-looking entrance. But the building is silent and shuttered, and I cannot tell what it used to be.

It is like being in a city at the bottom of the sea. There is only very little light left, in the evening sky. There is not even a whisper of any wind in the trees over my head.

But when, suddenly, some bus passes the entrance to the street where I stand, the whole corridor of silence between the tall walls of the houses fills up with the roar of air raids. I am ready to drop my suitcase and run for a cellar. My eyes hunt wildly in the dusk for the sign "Abri," and then the bus has vanished (the one sign of life: it was jammed with passengers). The noise subsides.

I am lost in the artificial city. The place is like something I have dreamed up, in bed, in the early hours of the morning when dreams are most vivid.

I start to walk. I come to the awning of a café. There is a concrete space where tables should stand: there are no tables. The blinds are down over the windows. There is a little light coming through a crack under one of the shades.

So I try the door of the café, and it opens.

Inside, all the chairs are piled on top of the tables, although it is only nine o'clock at night. This is the way it used to be at dawn. Only one bare bulb shines, over a pale white empty table where a group of seven or eight Frenchmen sit huddled together with their hats on their heads.

They turn to me like thieves, ready, with alibis and menaces, for the questions of the plain-clothes detective. But I see the expressions of defensiveness vanish from one face after another when the men realize that I am no detective, no German. Only the menaces remain. Fierceness hardens in all the eyes. Violence shines in their sights like diamonds. Two or three customers slowly stand up. A man with a mustache cries out as sharp as a gunshot:

"Et alors?"

The words race around the empty room. The challenge drops in this well of silence like a stone.

Even though this is a menace, I could laugh with happiness to hear it: by this I know I am in France: here is a word of true French. The men stand there with a strictly human and French anger in their eyes, offended, not like dogs, offended like men. I had thought human indignation had vanished from the face of the earth, leaving only the snarling of animals or the judgments of hypocrites.

I ask for the one hotel I remember in this quarter, the Hôtel Rocamadour, which must be somewhere near. I have wandered among the darkened wineshops and empty épiceries for an hour, trying to find it. The man with the mustache tells me in four words. Two other men, with caps, sit down again. But all their eyes still watch me, right out the door.

A light shines palely through the glass door of that little

hotel, which is at once the same and different from what I remember of it. I enter. The hall is much smaller than I expected. It is merely a little space, with a sort of a desk, less a desk than a schoolmaster's podium, stuck right at the bottom of the carpeted stairs.

The porter is a taciturn and bowlegged man, a Celt from the country of volcanoes in the center of France where the Gauls were driven by the Frankish invaders, and where the French have run to make their makeshift capital, among the iron casinos, the Third Empire Baths, and the quiet, slightly antiquated hotels.

I follow this Auvergnat up the stairs, this Helot. I remember the wide hats and the bagpipes and the black rocks crowned with huge statues of the Blessed Virgin, down in his cold green country. He does not speak. Maybe does not know how.

He takes me to a room at the top of the house, leaves without a word. I hear him go slowly down the stairs. I try to close the door but do not succeed until after several attempts. Finally it stays closed. I lock it, to keep it that way.

Without opening my bag, without moving my typewriter case from where the Celt has left it in the middle of the room, and without taking, in a glass, some of the stale water full of pinheads of old air in the carafe, I lie down on the bed, tired.

The naked bulb glares into my eyes. I close them. The city, the hotel, the bed become unbelievable. Madame Gongora, sitting in the sun, at Cannes, with the sea behind her, says:

"God no! Not Russian! Je te jure que je ne suis pas Russe! Gar nicht, caro! Ultramontana! South terre! Stamm' aus Sauveterre! Y Yo naci con mis parientes en el barrio de San Salvador, el mas hermoso de la capital de Casa!"

Then she slowly vanishes like a face in a movie, and I begin to hear this song:

The moon smiles like a queen,
(says the voice in my vision)
The star sings in the gate,
(shines the speech in my ear)
The waves all clap hands
(says the voice in my vision)
And the sleeping capes
(shines the speech in my ear)
Awake as shrill as children,
The sleeping capes awake as innocent
as children, lifting up their
Hands to high heaven,
(says the voice in my vision).
The queen of light comes shining like a ship.
The green hills sing hymns.
The rocks cry out like glass.
Leviathan plays in the gates of the ocean.
The man on the mast cries land!
(shines the speech in my ear)
The man on the mast cries land!

Then I sit up on the bed because the detectives are battering on my door.

They are big, thick-necked brutal men, Frenchmen that look and behave exactly like Germans. Their hats are too small for their big heads, and their pants are too tight for their fat asses, and too narrow and too short at the bottoms. On their feet, big, squeaking boots.

The first one confronts me:

"Vos papiers!"

The second one begins roaming around the room, looks under the pillow, lifts up my coat and weighs it for the weight of a gun.

"Why did you not leave your papers at the desk when you arrived?" says the first detective.

I didn't know, I forgot. Nobody reminded me.

The policeman takes, one by one, as I hand them to him, all my documents.

"This is my League of Nations passport," I say as I give him the first of the batch. He does not laugh. He makes no ironic remark. His expression does not change.

He is the kind of official to whom all documents, even meaningless, are objects of holy reverence. There can be nothing ridiculous or comical about an official document. It has to be either holy or a sacrilege, but can never be a cause of laughter.

"And this," I say, "is my Bolivian passport, which I bought last year for a hundred dollars in Havana."

"You have no need to give us your life history," says the flic. "Just give us your documents. We'll judge the rest. Where's your permit to travel around, and change from one arrondissement to another in Paris? Where's your permit to be in Paris at all?"

"Here," I say, "freshly forged."

To tell the unequivocal truth to an official like this is almost to tell a lie. Is it not a lie to say a thing in such a way that, to the person to whom you talk, not the truth but what is untrue is communciated? But these officials naturally assume that you mean the opposite to what you say. Therefore, if I tell them my permit is a fake, which is true, they will interpret that to mean it is not false but genuine, and I am only acting shifty.

I know how they will interpret my answer, and yet I go ahead and tell them this barefaced truth! How ashamed I immediately am! I could bite out my tongue! I have lied by telling the truth, because, to politicians and detectives and lawyers and judges, the truth only communicates a lie. If I desired to make clear that my permit was faked, I should make that quite clear by claiming it was genuine. It is too late. And now I give him also my pilot's license, my permit to carry money, my (totally false) permit to write this journal, and my revolver permit.

"And the revolver?" he says sharply.

"A Colt. I think I have lost it. I don't remember whether I packed it or not. I am always losing the thing. I wouldn't know how to use it anyway."

"Get that revolver out at once."

I open my suitcase and rummage around. I finally find the gun, in its holster, wrapped up in some soiled linen.

I lift it out of the suitcase.

"Stop," barks the detective, and I notice both of them have me covered with their own guns.

"Go on, throw it on the bed. You can't get away with that stuff!"

I throw the gun on the bed and cannot help laughing.

"Trying to shoot your way out, eh?" says one of them. "How many more guns have you got in that bag?"

"I've a mind to turn you in," says the first one. But the second one is crying out sharply:

"Ah! Ah! Ah! Ah! Vous voyez! Vous voyez! Hein!"

He has handfuls of paper: the manuscript of my journal, letters to and from my friends, to Madame Gongora.

"A communist!" says the first detective. "I think we are going to be very interested in these documents!"

Then they take everything that I have given them, and the journal besides. The door slams. I take out my typewriter from its case and load it with two sheets of paper and a carbon. And I write:

LETTER TO MADAME GONGORA

HOTEL ROCAMADOUR, PARIS

"O Cara Madama!

"Impressions of an event! Detectivos francesis, alligatos cum geheimnis-staps-polissongs, barran la puerta comes tonnerre getrommel, and scrammen down the giddy escalier with a periculous rattle of floor boards. Pieces of plaster and bits of ceiling and flakes of wall are falling in a shower from every quarter of my albergo. They got all my books and letters. Everything.

"Pobre mi! Verlores mik in Parisi, la bille lemure, la ville demeure, la vieille lumière, and what do you suppose? Lumineuse demeure fatta ahora negra, y mon moi senza passaportu (que me moco di esos) sino mas importante: sinza journelli. Carap! Some idiosyncrasy!

"Thus I have clicked and clattered into the deads of nocto many months past descripting the informacaos in multiple codes and invented double-talks: what is my identification with the guerra? And now they will try to figure out from that. Imaggini vos, tu illuminativa musatrix (for such you are, madama)(free lunches of information offered liberally to the reader at this point).

"And what do they find that youse have taught me to spik?

"Why, I am classed as a depayessed habitanto of some further demeure. Where's my house? Vid. Sup. What's my room number? Loc. Cit. I am a citoyen of a quite irreconcilable paysage, a voyageur among the citroens of terre, and on the highways and byways of the terrestrial globe I sells my cheap pearls of double-talky witsdom to nobody that won't have it. (There's your chance, you old established firms, who have been selling to the publics dumpses snipwit volumes of pure alligator between the bindings of Gosh! Money!) What fine and perplexed commerce is there, my sweet, doulce madama, Imperatrix Musaeorum, when now the smoky imaginations of the public detectives, hired to do in the open what the Germans do not hesitate to do in secret, spy on my unpublished works!

"Soon I shall aspire to a public of court recorders, and I shall be noncommercially present among the faked testifications of criminals. This is the way the trueman's justice gets itself wedged into print, far from the haunts of honest men, and maddened in the crowds of crooky lip speeches, in the dank and dust of legal (sipsup) chicanery. Nice use of the word clicky. Thus, at last, I am read.

"Far from the milk of the muse, I thirst in the Armistice days of a foreign city, mad with the absolute silence of conquest. Madama, read in your book of St. John's of the Cross and tell me what not to say. Meanwhile I proceed in the same old worldly terms. I am so unpublished, I am a kind of a Trappist, in my own way. I am so kept apart from the thirsting imaginations of the public not unintelligent but greedy for such books as I think I want to write (all about God in a new witty and pertinent way, face first through the muck of the reeky civilization we got ourselves stuck with, and out of the other side with double-talk in my hair like a swimmer free of the weeds!) that I am a kind of Trappist.

"I have written double-talk under the aspect of a kind of vow of silence, I guess, and that is anyway what it turns out to be. But it is honest, darling. That is the way I invite your inspirations, madama, living in your otherworldly house, not out of the bombed city, not in the eighteenth century, not in the sentimental minds of the moralizing communists, but in and out of the world, knowing the illusion from the truth. Teach me, teach me. Don't be afraid to write me a card, now and then!

"The late religious Joyce was a blaspheming man. He lost his Catholic faith and was cruel to his mother. His pride was as hard as a stone and he smelled hell every day of his life, what with all he had to go through, poor blind man! But he was one of the best I can think of, and all I pray is he shall come to the place of saints, for he was an honest writer. Throw the beams out of your eyes, youse who hope to be in heaven: if Joyce was so smutty, then pray for him, as we were told to do in the paysage where we want to get back.

"Imaginni vos la escena. It is the estazao di polizi. Tienen mis papiruses, and all my Trappist charters and my vow-of-silence noncommercial speeches and my Esperanto prayers because I am too unable to write any other way and feel clean. How will the detectives climb the rungs of my proverbial sentences like what follows:

> Toute lettera se fait un Jacob's Ladder,
> Hasta el ciel, desde la lousy terre:
> Laquelle habemos, con nos vils orgueils
> Hecho la casa di folor y guerre!

"This is my theory of prints and impresses and scribbles and codexes, and you might as well use it for a colophon because you won't get much else, to start with (not you, madama: these others here, these three or four readers).

"Now the sergeant of the polizi plucks up my rhodo-montadoes. Now he claps his hand to his hat. Now he bats his flying tears away from his eyes, and scatters his moans of anguish around the courtrooms where the rain falls alike upon the just and the righteous.

"Is this semicelestial Esperanto or is it odd for odd's sake? Don't ask Sergeant; he's drenching his head in a pail and yelling for an aspirin.

"And the only other thing is: I wish everything I wrote would be able to be read most of all by children and nuns and holy people, but there I know I am crazy to expect that, because I have trailed around in the dirt too much to please them, they are happy and good, and talk straighter than I because they haven't got so much pride to try to work into humility one way and another.

"Mientras nosotros revassam, dormido, de nuevo, after the terrors of the nokto, revassemos en nuestro lecho di

Provenza, di nuestro sommeil casi Catalan (di Catalan im-
maginar!), diciendo:

> Dans su journelle el escribi
> Scribe los fatos de lo giovedi,
> Scribe memoria de Dominica
> Y otras cosas que en mente ha.
>
> Refleji en su cor de tecnico
> Su tipo de poema favoritt:
> Et es el tipo macaronico
> Lo mas hermoso jamais que se vitt!
>
> Porque sta notte no si scrive more?
> Di medianoche suena nuu die Hore
> Cuando se fa preghieras, va al lecho
> Y duerme con sus holy medals spread across his pecho.

"Buona nuotte, Musatricce! Ahora torno to some otra
speeches, make my kneels on the cold earth, turn my face
to my palms, and speak: Salve Regina, Mater misericordiae,
vita, dulcedo et spes nostra, salve: ad te clamamus, exsules
filii Hevae: ad te suspiramus gementes et flentes in Paris,
France, 1941, etc."

XX

HOTEL ROCAMADOUR
PARIS

French detectives are the worst. They have got my journal, the journal in the language of Casa. The honest' poet's journal: honest's Esperanto. I lie in my tin bed. All night half awake. Assoupi. Poet lies in his tin bed, Assoupi.

The room is full of water. The poet's mind swims in the quiet gray water of a half-waking dream. The water of my rêves, pli, repli, pli, repli. Water folds around the thoughts of the poet, unfolds, folds. Pli.

Paris is full of 1909 movies that flicker like an old gray storm of rain: that is how the poet sees the Paris of the German conquest. The animated black and white Germans jig-jig through the flashing movie of that ancient rainstorm before I was born.

The poet lies on his tin bed. Germans jig on the cinema walls, the bathyspheric windows of the poet's bedroom. Dreams!

The poet's mind is full of the sternest German maps, developing cinematographically to explain this dream of Paris, on the walls and ceiling, in the flooded tanks of the Hôtel Rocamadour.

Europe swims and expands, in pictures, according to

the subtle methods of the propaganda film. The shape of Germany in white shines surrounded by the shapes of all Europe in black. Music plays. The maps of the countries swell and fade and swell, divide and swim in their curious, unintelligible dance.

Little pointed flags march out of Germany's map, in every direction, point outward and cut their way through all the black fantasy, march primly in the confusion of the big dividing shapes. Soon the map of Germany makes a bigger, neater shape, devouring, purifying all the others, making all Europe light, white, one. Manifest destiny!

The voice of the commentator is muffled by the waters that fill the tank the poet sleeps in, but he hears:

"Caro populi inferior. Explanation de nuestro conquisti sobre vous. Ensuite. Du calme. Sleep, poeta! Swim, scribu, dans su acuario tan curios, di rêves. Begin!"

The poet stirs, crying out, in the creak of his bed, a prisoner in the dream. He feels the drag of the cords that tie down his wrists to two great weights. He feels the weight of the rocks to which he is fettered at the ankles. He is imprisoned in the midst of the frightful calm of the commentator's voice.

"Caro populi inferior. Good big German love you plenty. Trop gentil: caresse, ou bien scraack plaf schibogenmord stutz kampf schmakken todt. Achtung. Aleman vous liebt. Trop gentil. You better like it!

"Now in the very earliest years of the eighteenth century it is understandable that, owing to the inevitable, due to our never-to-be-misunderestimated Frederick the Gross, surnamed Gross, expansion, the Reich, beloved, the Poles, adjacent, summarily divided has, up.

"Tolerably the small, intolerable as great, from futile recrimination, over a period of years, desists. Despite the offers of amistad le mas cordial, handshakken, regalo de flowers and candy, cigari, cigaretten, pipes, toffee, caramelo, peanuts, cocoa, parfumo, etc., etc., nuestro trahissable petit vecino, fiendishly consumato mit dem diplomatik from the degenerato popolo Inglesi-Franco, hasslich the hand that held the coated candy, unscrupulous, bites, and himself to the Dutches Rig upoveragainst aroused ist.

"The tooth that licked the boot that handed the gentlest biscuit kindness could devise in the labor of love has lashed the unhelmeted cheek of the friend with the most unholy traitor's bludgeon and left in searing brand the sobriquet 'You gave us no biscuits, like you said, at all!'

"Then scrapes up an excuse for a unified republic decked out in the cast off feathers of that last rose of the paleolithic summer, dark Albion, promist bombardieren nuestro Berlini (O alas, hororis!), nuestro Dresdeni, nuestro Hedelburgo tan cultural! O sopor what a blinding grief to be thus twanged by the whiptooth of an ingrate voisin, rejetant nos caramels in favor of the pastilles valda of the friendless French.

"And thus, caro populo inferior, se poda vedir la necesidado de borombaradadar (gently of course) cum flammenwerfer y todo, completi, vuestro insignificante pais!"

The cinematic maps in the sleepless mind of the poet flash and flicker with a hundred thoroughly commonplace lights in order to suggest the compromise that ensued. Much picturesque! Que confusio, tan illuminado, tan electrique! And so the restless movies of history proceed to no satisfying conclusion whatever, and the poet, in his tin bed, turns over and cries in the night.

Now I am awake again, completely. I rise up in the tangled sheets and put my feet on the floor. I don't know what time it can be. (I never carry a watch.) It is the depth of night, but I do not think the conquered city is asleep, even then. There are noises in the hotel, as if people might be speaking, somewhere, just out of hearing, just too far away for you to make out the sound of voices. But there is some sound, everywhere.

I throw open the windows on the blacked-out city and am surprised to see the sky is full of stars. I look out over the roofs of the city that was only really raided once, and that in the middle of the day.

And now I lean on the sill of this room's window, where I am supposed to be imprisoned, and look at the dark roofs and the stars.

I remember all the nights I was ever awake, in France, when I was a child.

The windows of the Lycée's infirmary looked out over the tiled roofs of a suburb of Montauban. There was a white wall, that already looked destroyed, between the Lycée and the street. Over there, somewhere, southward, on the edge of the yellow bluff this part of the town stood on, was the Gothic spire of a new church, overlooking the small square full of stunted plane trees where they guillotined the murderers from the town's prison. Beyond that, the bluff fell to the plains where the Tarn River ran. Out there was emptiness, wood smoke, vineyards, the dark and violent night, the house of the bishop, the barracks of the African troops.

And from those barracks, a fierce, outlandish Islamic bugle would blow, so that I shivered, where I lay, in my infirmary bed. I used to lie awake and listen to the sounds of the South of France outside that bare window, and beyond the ruined wall. A distant train, beyond the river, shrieking with its high-pitched and forlorn whistle. Far off in the town a harshly clanging church bell that rings rapidly and stops all of a sudden, in some brick tower.

Later on, when the night became totally silent, I was still awake in this high, lonely infirmary room. I waited, now for the slippered, half-audible approach of the night watchman along the hall outside, going his rounds. When he came, through the little glass window, in the middle of the door of my ward, the light of his lantern would shine and cast a wildly swinging rectangle of light all over the ceilings and the crazy walls, and his footsteps would go by and the light would disappear, and the sound of his slippers on the linoleum would die away. Then, somewhere in the building, a door would slam, and the slam would echo through the empty corridors to my bed in the infirmary.

All around me, from that ward, in the infirmary, spread the Lycée in every direction in long brick wings two stories high. In these were some dormitories, part empty (for the place was only half full), part full of iron beds where lay the peasant children of the South in their tough sleep, lean, hard, mean kids full of violence, strange humor, and rhetoric.

In the morning they would stand in the gravel yards of the Lycée in groups, in their black smocks, and taunt one another fiercely, and pull each other's ears, and twist them until they nearly wrenched them from each other's heads.

Now I think of them in the mud of the prison camps, in Germany, wild, disgusted men, standing with their hands in their pockets, no longer talking, no longer sticking out their heads and their chins at one another with their clanging rhetoric, their kniving accusations. Now they stand silent and walk about with none of the furious noise that used to fill the courtyards of the Lycée, when they used to tear each other's ears off. Because now they are prisoners, now they are nearly dead of homesickness for that stony red earth in Languedoc, for those dusty little villages where the farms were all falling to pieces, those hills crazy with zig-zags of vineyard, those red church towers with their harsh bells, those velodromes, those football grandstands covered with corrugated iron.

Now they are standing looking out, through the electrified wire, at the dead sky of a country they hate.

That is the way it is, in the world, all of a sudden. There were years of uncertainty when anything might happen and you argued until you suddenly sickened, in the pit of the stomach, and stopped for disgust. Then the regiments were called up; you had scarcely done your military service and you were called back. Then you waited some more and argued some more. Then everything went crazy. Everything inside and outside your head began to explode. It was as if the universe was being thrown right at you. Then you came to and you were living in the midst of these wires in a gray world, and everything had stopped and was standing still.

The nervous world had sorted itself out, and everybody was standing still, in groups. There was no more movement, no more argument, no more instability. Finished. Everybody was in prison, wired up in pens, penned up in fields, herded together in the mud, forever. It was as bad as being dead, but less comprehensible.

And you no longer knew anything. Maybe this was the true state of nature, to be penned in a wire pen, and stand still, and rot, with all words dead in your throat and all emotion turned to a sickness under the heart.

You, by the waters of Babylon, sit down and weep in Germany, you prisoners of war, and the poet leans on the sill of his window, and looks at this city, all dark, full of secret unidentifiable noises: the poet, by the waters of Babylon, in the blacked-out city.

The voice of the commentator begins again:

"Caro populi inferior. Big German love you plenty. Caressen, blandieren, ami, trop gentil! Restez tranquille, poète. Pour eux, c'en est déjà assez!"

XXI

ABANDONA pigrizij: ESCAPO!
Yherezt nopitty ont dzhe steirs.
Dzhere eitz nobbudy onz dhe stoirs.
L'auvergnat est parti. Descendumos.
(Next floor. Still nobody.)
Jzhere idz nyubbodi omn dlhe shtiars.
Where is the auvergnat? Whu yar yuh, crubble? Hiding?
Tzere its noobodo uan we stairs, nope. Non.
Où est il, ce petit crapule? Où te caches tu?
(Et iss onlee tzhe catt!)
Dear has nopretty in the stars? Bear his no baby at the
stares. Dzhere is . . . Ah! C'est l'auvergnat!
Nope, thzere is knobbodi, et ul.
Descendumi, piccolo ceri, mon vero, descendimo, escape
mientras el si fuo, pendant que is in the stairs nullo, nip:
no pod.
Es il? Vient? Around that corner? Il guette, le salaud.
Il m'attend. Attrappe! Malotru! Es il? Le vendu?
Et iss onlee, the catt, egein.
Dzhere ess know's doddy on these stairs, nope.
One more flight. We creak, we sing like a piece of lame

complaining of the wind in the tree. We sing like a hinge. We cry out like a joint in the bone.

Where are youse, you bent double? you little rended voyou? Waiting for me behind all the doors, with the police?

Fazemos nuestro escapo, providenti no vide nos el janitori.

On a dark night in the middle of the afternoon, when my hotel was all at rest, there was nobody in the stairs. They slept for starvation, the paid crapules of the shifty Dutch, the parties to my imprisonment in this my present world of life and time, my hotel being now at rest. How I long to go!

On a dark night in the middle of the afternoon in July 1941 I dreamed I escaped from the Hôtel Rocamadour, where I was prisoned in Paris by all the forces inimical to my salvation. And I dreamed there was nobody on the stairs, in my dream, but that I must go cautiously in the stairs, for fear the Auvergnat might be behind one of the doors, hiding, with my enemies the French police, or worse, the Gestapo, who have not yet come to catch me, my hotel being now at rest.

Abandona pigrizij:

The silent windows open like mouths, the locked doors suddenly stare like eyes, the stair well cries like a voice: "Abandona Pigrizij, up, vero Christian, Escapo, ESCA-PO-O-O!"

(The word rings in the echoing stair well.)

On a dark night, when my hotel was all at rest, in the middle of the afternoon, all Paris was dying slowly of starvation, and there was nobody in the stairs to prevent my escape, yet going down the stairs was like a whole lifetime.

Who is waiting before me around the corner of the passageway, upon the worn-out carpet that is nailed into the nineteenth-century silence of this floor? Who is waiting for me, behind the frosted glass doors, so gray? My hotel being now at rest: Oh, escapo-o.

What foot moves the board of that hall floor? What hand brushes the whitewashed plaster wall? What there, O, what? Runs?

Only the cat.

What stirs the leaves of the calendar, saying: "Cassis"? It is the wind under the street door. The bell shines on the desk; there is no hand to strike it. The wind, unseen, flies over the shining surface of the bell and strikes no sound.

The flight to the ground floor is the longest flight of all: what if they have waited there behind to let me pass them by, and one by one now follow me in the stairs, my hotel being now at rest?

On a dark, in the middle of the afternoon, night, escapo-o de mi hotel, estando ya mi casa sosegada.

Pray for me, St. John of the Cross, to get through that door, where the air comes under, where the light shines through, my house being now at rest. On a dark night.

Dzhere iss nobodi et dzhe ground flor dour.

Jzhere esz now putti ed jye crown flowcr tur.

Sayhr iss noputi ett yeh creon fleor teor.

Ay Out! Oot! Uit! Vit'l Escapo-o-o!

Clama lo escaloir di subito grossi vacarmi, est els, vinen!

Betrayed! Flogged by the cops! They've come!

On all sides, roar like bulls, roar like trains, the fat bulls, the roarers in the stairs, which roars with the shouts of the police like the sound of electric bells, like the sound of accidents at the corners of streets, like the sound of the demolition of buildings, like the sound of air raids, like the sound of thunder, in the well of the stairs, my house being not at rest:

They are in the doors, the two detectives, the doors they have suddenly flung open in their accusation below me, and behind me, above me, are the Auvergnat and the rest of the police, my house being not at rest, I run upward, I turn, I cannot run downward, I turn.

The stairs neigh like horses, the stairs neigh like the exclamation "Ay-y-y!" The stairs throw back their neighing into the top of the house and out the skylight into the unbelievable sky while the detectives cry out echoing:

"Atrapo! Halti! Volur! Spione! Ha toujur ke faire cum nous! Atrapo! Halta! Fujitiv! Escapantor! Arreste!"

Atrapdo por lis crapuls. O remedia, no, helas, null

"Halto! Arreste!"

The detectives from below advance one step into the doorway and the doors swing closed; they stand at the bottom of the stairs. I thought my house was at rest. I am caught.

On a dark night, in the middle of the afternoon, I dreamed I was about to escape from the Hôtel Rocamadour, where I am kept prisoner, but it was only a dream.

I get off the bed in my room and walk across the floor, with the words of the empty stair well in my ears, the dream heavy in my head like an earful of water, and I walk, still deaf and drunk, to the window, and throw it open and breathe the air, and look at the sky. It is cloudy, I am sorry, for my whole life.

I put on my shoes and socks, like a man who has been hit in the mouth. I brush my hair like a man who has been knocked down. The dream is as thick in my head as the noise of a train in a tunnel.

But the other thing is that if I cannot escape from the hotel in my dream, I am perfectly free to walk in and out of the one I sleep and dream in, anytime I like. I have been given the permission of the police to leave my hotel, but I must be back by night, and I must not leave before dawn. I can go and come as I please, but only by day. This is not a dream, nor a myth. I cannot get out of here in my dream, but I can when I am awake. I have been given what seems to be liberty.

I stand up like a man who has been hit with a pillow. The dream seeps out of my ear like water and my head clears.

I stand at the top of the stairs, and there is, indeed, nobody in the stairs. I lock my door like a free man, from the outside. I walk down the stairs thinking of the dream. It is true, there is nobody in the stairs.

However, it is also true that when I get to the bottom of the stairs, there will be nothing outside the door, except only the street.

It is already nothing new to me to walk out into the street and hear my real feet on the stones. The street is in the present, not in the past, not in a dream.

(In the past, when my father and I came out of the Hôtel Rocamadour, perhaps fourteen years ago, when he carried his suitcase, which, when opened, smelled of artist's paint and tobacco, then we took the train for the South that went through Orléans and over the wide red Loire, and past Limoges on the bluff, and among the poplars, through Brive la Gaillarde and Cahors, where the country got stony and fierce, and we would be home.

This is no longer that street, where I walked then, starting out from the Hôtel Rocamadour to go to the Quai d'Orsay station. It is another street, in the present.)

It has other associations.

The other day I came out to go to the police.

I shall recall what happened, when I was summoned by the detectives, at the Hôtel Rocamadour, and led off to the investigation from which, to my great surprise, I emerged more or less free to go about in Paris as I pleased.

First, we had to walk through the streets empty of cars to the Ile de la Cité. We went in silence. The detectives would, obviously, be distrustful of anything I might say, and any innocent, friendly remark might, after having been

turned over and over in their slow and suspicious imaginations, be perverted into something sinister against me.

Besides, I had nothing to say, and they, of course, didn't
have any more to say than I had.

I particularly remember one of them, because he was one
of those Frenchmen that look exactly like Germans (there
are quite a few), big, bullish, thick-necked, heavily mustached, dewlapped under the jowl with fat flesh, looking
always angry, humorless, and mortally offended by the universe.

All the way along the river, on the empty quays, I men-
tally compared the bigger of the two detectives that ac-
companied me with first Monsieur Lindemann, an Alsatian
with all the worst instincts of not only the German but the
French bourgeoisie, who was a retired chef and lived in the
rooms beneath us, between the river and the Cattle Market
in St. Antonin, and, second, with Monsieur Lanne, who was
one of the supervisors at the Lycée, and who sat, huge, on his
high podium while all around the room the children sor-
rowed in the pale electric light.

I can't remember in what way Lanne and Lindemann
looked different, if they did at all. The detective looked like
them both.

Where are you now, old Lindemann, not that I care? Your
wife and you would cough loud, angry artificial coughing
in your bed when we walked over your heads in the night,
and when the coughing didn't do any good, we could hear
you banging under our feet with a broomstick on your ceiling, our floor.

Where are you now, old Lanne, crouching in your tower
with the newspaper, and brooding at the room, over the
heads of the mean, sad, clever children whom you hated?

Where are you now, old Lindemann, standing in the hall
of your house, giving orders to your small, furtive wife, and
bowing to my father, speaking the words of English you

learned as a waiter, giving yourself the airs you picked up as a householder, talking, so, half insolent and half servile, half waiter and half field marshal, while we go down the stairs to get away from your heavy wit?

The German-French detective walks beside me, Lindemann and Lanne. I am half inclined to ask him if he was ever a waiter, if he knows any waiter's English (so far he has only talked to me in French, when he has talked at all).

The other detective is nothing at all, walks like a man brooding over some fierce, inward sickness, and really has no traits at all, discernible from the outside. To know him, you would perhaps have to get a list of the patent medicines and the mineral waters and the tisanes and medicinal wines he takes for his health.

We cross the bridge, and I notice that there are many men in ragged clothes standing along the banks and on the idle stones, holding fishing rods, waiting for the little gray fish, that taste as dirty as the Seine, to tug lightly on the end of their lines. But the barges that used to be tied along the stone quays are gone, whether to the coast, to carry soldiers to England, as the papers say, or only out of the way to make papers say that, nobody knows. There are no more barges.

We enter the long, straight street that leads up to the Palais de Justice. It is more like a street in Germany than any other street in Paris, and suddenly I remember that it really is a street in Germany.

There is a strange and deadly regularity about the buildings, as if they were all the same height, down both sides of the street, and then, on the pavement, I hear the loud footsteps of German soldiers coming toward us.

The courtyard is Germany. Soldiers stand on the steps. At the foot of the steps is an officer's car, waiting for the officer to come out. All around, rows and rows of windows look down coldly from the black walls. The building was built to accommodate such soldiers and such officers. The building is perfectly content.

We go up and inside and start walking through the corridors, interminable as the corridors of lycées and prisons. Far down at the other end, a bareheaded German soldier comes out of a door with a brief case under his arm, comes toward us for a certain distance; but before he gets anywhere near us, he opens another door and disappears into it, leaving the slam to echo down the halls toward us.

Then we come to the room where I am to be questioned.

Two detectives sit over at the side of the room, with hats on and their arms folded. The ones with me make signs for me to sit on a bench.

Who will come out of the door, at the other end of the room? The little, narrow-eyed censeur of the Lycée, with his wispy red mustache?

What will the censeur say?

He will take from my hands the thin, cheap paper novels that I have just sadly bought in the street leading down to the river, in Montauban, fourteen years ago. I will say meekly:

"I believed it was permitted to read these books, since they are considered to be good literature."

He will reply:

"They will be returned to you when you go home."

"What is the matter with these books?" I ask humbly.

"They will be returned to you when you go home."

By the time I go home, I will have forgotten all about them, and I never read those books, two novels of Pierre Loti, one about a sailor in the French Navy, and now that I remember them for the first time in years I have no longer any desire to read them.

Who will come out of the door?

The little censeur of the Lycée, with his thin, wispy mustache and his eyes slanting like a Chinaman's, but his skin as pale as a Russian's: he must have been some kind of a Mongol. He was little and fierce, and everybody was afraid of him because he could keep us in, on Sundays, the day we were allowed to roam in the town, and read *Match*, and go to the movies, and buy candy and smoke cigarettes and go to the rugby games in the suburbs.

What will he ask me?

He might ask me what I am afraid of. I am afraid of the cold walls of the corridors in the Lycée. I am afraid of the gravel in the playgrounds, and of the sickly smell of the blossoming acacias in the spring. I am afraid of getting water on my knee, because when you have water on the knee they lance your knee. I am afraid of the sound of the harsh church bells, ringing in the distant town, outside the walls. I am afraid of the rain that rained all winter so that the river flooded the suburbs, and raced under the bridges, filling up their arches, carrying away trees and dead cattle.

He will ask me why I fear the dark room where they teach mathematics. He will ask me why I didn't believe the fierce boys when they told me that the guillotine where the murderers were beheaded was always set up behind the Lycée, and that the next morning, about the time we awoke at dawn, one might be able to hear the knife fall with a clang, behind the walls. He will ask me why I fear the little Protestant chapel built like an empty blast furnace in one of the courts—a forge where all the fires have gone out.

I sit and stare at the white, proud, paranoiac bust of the Republic with her Phrygian cap, that stands in the niche in the wall. I stare at the letters RF and the fasces and the laurel crown. The halls of the Palais de Justice ring like the corridors of the Lycée, where the barking of the boys was sharp, like foxes' in the cold air of January mornings, and where the steps of the censeur and the proviseur, walking side by side on tours of inspection, fell on the stones like the ticking of a big, inexorable clock.

Then, under the pale, fanatical bust of the freethinking Republic, the door opens, and in comes a thin-faced Frenchman with a nervous, uniformed German. They both sit down behind the high desk together and talk in low voices without looking up, until suddenly the Frenchman looks over at me and says impatiently:

"Et bien, approchez vous, approchez vous!"

The room is silent. The sound of leaves of paper, being turned over and over by the hands of the Gestapo official, is like knives.

"This document," begins the Frenchman quietly, holding up several pages of my journal, which was taken from me by the detectives, "in what does it consist?"

"It is a personal journal, with letters. It consists in notes on my own intimate experience; it consists in notes on memories that I don't understand and some that I worry about."

"Then this document, you declare under oath, consists in love letters?"

"No, it does not consist in love letters, it consists in personal reflections."

"That is what I said: mémoires galantes?"

"No, no, it is nothing but a book of meditations on my life, my memories."

"Precisely," says the official, "smutty souvenirs."

The German raises his hand, demanding a little quiet in the court. Then he says to me:

"I find this book is filled with communist-capitalist prose. How do you explain that?"

I am left speechless.

"Don't you understand me? I say: your book is written in communist-capitalist prose! Answer me! Is that true?"

I cannot say a word. The German officer tightens up like a spring: I do not know what he is going to do next, break in fifteen pieces like a glass full of boiling tea, or merely burst into tears.

"Do you understand me?" he shouts.

I can only shake my head.

Then the German roars out:

"Bring the interpreters!"

Four or five men in shabby coats, and one in a French soldier's uniform, come in. It is immediately apparent that the soldier is no longer on active duty; he is an unemployed soldier picking up some money as interpreter. He is brushing his hands together, shaking the crumbs of a roll from the skirts of his coat, for I gather that the interpreters were enjoying a little breakfast in the other room, and glad to get it, by their looks!

"Now, talk!" shouts the officer.

"Si, uffizir!"

"Ask this man why his book is written in communist-capitalist prose."

All the interpreters turn to me at once and begin to babble together.

"One at a time!" shouts the German. Then, picking out the soldier, he says:

"You, you question this man. Why is his book written in communist-capitalist prose?"

The soldier turns to me and, with his back to the officer, makes a comical face, rolls his eyes, and says:

"Ah, figure toi, mon vious, el uffizi, qua, se dement', ah, le pauv' cocu; vult saper che cosa, moi, sabes, no comprenni di nada lou que el se express con su manieri di explosao. Well, que pens, que voy lui responsir?"

"Lo ke tu desiris, amigou! Moi je n'y comprends rien non plus."

The soldier turns to the German officer and replies:

"Prince, the man says he merely writes memorandums, no more."

"The prose, the prose, the communist-capitalist prose," shouts the officer, "question him concerning his style."

"Tu vois," says the soldier to me, "le v'là encore qui se démène comme un enragé. Qu'est-ce qui'l veut dire, prose communiste-capitaliste? Quoi, il est détraqué? Qu'est-ce que je vais lui répondre?"

"Dis lui que c'est de la mathématique. Il est Allemand, il ne sait pas lire: il te croira!"

"Prince," says my friend, "the man says it isn't the kind of prose you say at all, but mathematics."

"Jewish mathematics, I'll be bound," says the officer. "Ask him that!"

"Furibondo," says my interpreter, "cognasse! Sclavo! Immondizi! Testa clavata, puzza di bestie, hombre, que ce drame empeste une merdeuse humeur allemande! Chico, me gustaría mucho flankan di colpo de peddibus por totas patris di su cuerpo bombástico-ballonitif; que se pasa nella testa cerebral di ce confuso fussbalspieler! Crikey, when he was young he must of fall out of a airplane, excuse the joke, but on his head. Et que veux tu que je lui dise?"

"Encore un coup, dis lui que c'est pas du juif, mais au contraire de la poésie runique."

"Chieftain," says my interpreter, "the sir claims his memoirs are nothing more or less than runic songs, old delicate ballads, in runes, fables of the Nordic twilight that even now blossoms into the Stygian blackness of infinite midnights of culture, all over the earth."

"Runes," says the German, "that's different, unless of course they're English runes, seeing that the English are all Jews, cowards, crapules, Winston Churchills, millionaires, dentists, fairies, aviators, boasters, hypocrites, bullies, fanatics, and beasts. Ask him if he is a fanatic."

"Atrapa lou que diss' ili nunco. Fanático! Y-lu mismo tan admirado del Afredi Hitler che, si possibli, volontieri mangerait su propria grossmutter."

"Mi estoufo de reir a carcajadas. Casi no puedo respiar, por estimulo comichissime di la vena risitive. I believe this boy is going to turn into windmills, he is so mad. Qu'est-ce que tu penses!"

"O alors!" says the interpreter, and swings around and says to the officer, who may or may not be the gauleiter of Paris, but I can't figure out just what he is: "O ring giver," says the interpreter, "the man avers he is a fanatic, yes, but only fanatical for the movies, for vegetable soups, for big fat German women, for crushing down the Polish upstarts, for despoiling the English and living forever and ever stuffed up with cream puffs and vulgarity to the end of time. He is just like you, master, honest, he swears he is."

"You expect me to believe a tissue of cowardly lies. If he isn't German, how can he aspire to be perfection? How can he long to live in a house as big and black as a big black beer hall with rings on his fingers and nine-pound heavy iron boots on his feet and gold teeth in his head and medals all over the pocket where he keeps his cigars? How can he long to live in a heaven of expensive body belts and big frowning stone dames and nineteenth-century under-wear, and paintings of women and serpents, and growl like a big, beautiful hog into his ten-gallon vessel of ersatz beer? Can he fast and strive in order to win himself, at long last, the most monstrous drunken stupor that was ever heard of in the history of men, let alone us handsome giants?"

So we talk back and forth, through the medium of this interpreter, who generally makes up more of the answers than I do: and all the while, it is going into the record of the court, if it is a court at all.

General: "If the suspect is civilized, why can't I under-stand his book?"

"Because it is private memorandums."

"Private memorandums are a sign of decadence and lu-nacy, the use of strange words is a perverted trick by the ruthless, fiendish littérateurs of the communist-capitalist cliques of Wall Street and the ghettos of Mayfair, in order to enrage, annoy, and try the patience of all clean, healthy younger races, at present being raped by the warmongering grocers, bank clerks, printers' apprentices, engineers' assistants, and accountants of the lunatic plutocracies. Where's the ideology in all these runes, as they are alleged to be, if not the encirclement and extermination of the shining white quivering bodies of our shrieking defenseless Aryan youth?"

Answer: "No, no, these are quite distinct. These are Aryan, lyric runes, the full song from the throat of the pre-Icelandic dawn. These are nothing more or less than pure Norse mathematics, laundry lists in old Gothic algebra, records of half-forgotten tea engagements with unimportant relatives reduced to old High German symbols from fact and fable, truth and fancy."

Question: "Where does it say in these runes that the Fuehrer is the salvation of the crushed peoples of poor, gigantic, defenseless Germany? Where does it praise our recent adoption of our Polish, Austrian, French, Greek, Ukrainian living rooms?"

Answer: "It is purely a nonpolitical diary."

Question: "Then if it is nonpolitical, non-Jewish, noncapitalistic, noncommunistic, what is it?"

Apparently the gauleiter, if he is the gauleiter, and if they have one in Paris, is simmering down as fast as he boiled up. The interpreter merely repeats, for me, that this is a personal journal.

The general, or we will call him gauleiter, pauses for a while, sighing and breathing deeply with the effort of some kind of thought that is going on in his head, and then says:

"Very well. If you foreigners were only less stupid and more subtle and refined in your way of expressing yourselves, you would have come out in the first place and admitted that this was a spicy book of personal memories."

The interpreter steps into the background. We are back

where we started. I come forward and humbly begin where
I began before:

"No, no, it is nothing but a book of meditations on my
life, my memories."

"Smutty souvenirs," says the officer. "It has taken us all
day to determine what the book is, but it is a book of smutty
souvenirs."

"But sir, I mean, Chieftain . . ."

"Do not try to confuse the issue with your own tortured
language that defines nothing," says the gauleiter. "I have
the whole thing defined in the simplest and clearest terms.
It is all settled. We will allow you to go. We will have the
immense bounty and patience to forget that the language and
content of your book are unfair, by implication if not overtly,
to the most beautiful, peace-loving people on earth. We are
willing to pass over in tactful silence the fact that your book
is a compendium of delicious, bawdy, Rabelaisian and Fal-
staffian drolleries that will bring a chuckle to faces that have
longed for weary months of sacrifices for a good, dirty laugh.

"Go," he continues, "and no longer try to hoodwink us:
we know you are a writer of luscious, cheap pornography.
Do not pretend to be what you are not. What you are is
shameful but at least tolerable. Runic, religious memorandums! Newspaper reporter! What do you think we Germans
are, fools?"

And all this while, the Frenchman is handing back to me,
with breathless respect for everything that the gauleiter is
saying, all my different passports, my gun, my tickets, my
permits, my passes, my identification, forged and real.

"You can get out," says the gauleiter, "but remember, this
is the last time you can come around here pretending to be
a German and get away with it. It is no use: you will never
be one. Count yourself lucky to be tolerated, dismissed with
only the mildest reproof, for all your private smut, because
you have blond hair and blue eyes in this country of carpet

salesmen, Mediterranean Jews, Smyrna fig merchants, and gibbering Ali Babas, the crude unfortunate French."

And with this he gets up and slams his hand down on the desk, and all the Frenchmen, all the detectives and the interpreters, and everybody in the room, except myself and the unemployed soldier, clap neatly like old ladies in a theater, and some purse their lips and cry:

"Bis! Bis! Bis! O, the indubitable charm of the chieftain's golden words, O, the unutterable truth of the little master's gorgeous and quasi-eternal wisdom, O, the blameless purity of his Germano-Gallic rhetoric that shows us poor muzhiks up to be the luckless churls that we now realize we are."

And outside, in the hall, I can still hear their applause, polite, prolonged, and shrill.

XXII

I come out of the Palais de Justice and turn down the street as if to start running, on the empty pavements, now that there are no detectives on either side of me. My feet turn to air, my heart flies upward like on the first day of a vacation, going to the station; and then immediately my feet turn to lead, my heart remains stone: it does no good to be free in this city, because freedom to move around is not the freedom I was looking for. I admit, for many people it would be enough to gain that freedom, and a terrible thing to lose it.

Only that is not what I am concerned with.

So I cross the branch of the river again.

Left Bank. Under my feet, somewhere here, the train runs that goes south. I never loved the Left Bank except for this, and maybe the Cluny Museum. I think of the tunnel leading along the river from the Gare d'Orléans.

In the gray cut, passing the Jardin des Plantes, the train moves slowly in the light of late afternoon, and we are going South. Everywhere in the third-class compartment people begin to open bottles of wine, false wine, it seems to me, because somewhere I picked up the prejudices of the South:

this is Paris wine, and Paris grows no wine of its own; it is false, imported wine. The brown-painted compartment smells of wine and bread and garlic, but it is all right, that is natural: maybe at sunset we will cross, at Orléans, the wide Loire, and see the twin, elaborate towers of the cathedral rising over the flat city.

I never fully believed in Paris, never worshiped Paris. I believed in Toulouse and Carcassone and Perpignan and Narbonne and Marseilles and Avignon, but I did not believe in the cities of the North.

Now that I am in this city, it does me no good to remember that I am free, because I never was free here, even when Paris was really free. I was always thinking of the train going South, under this embankment, or maybe on the other side of the Seine, and farther down, going toward Burgundy and Lyon and the Rhône.

I walk sadly along the quay, toward the Institut, under the trees.

A German officer is standing at one of the bookstalls. He is all alone. He looks wearily from one book to another and yet cannot tear himself away. He looks sadly over the stall, hunting from one title to another:

"Elie Faure, Georges Courteline, Henri Barbusse, the poems of André Chénier; Henri Bordeaux, François Coppée."

No wonder he is sad. He turns past me like a man who is sick, and walks away in the same direction as I, with his head down. He looks like one about to throw himself into the river.

Yet although he started ahead of me, he slows in his walk, until I soon pass him. I am afraid he might want to start talking, and he does. Just as I am past him, he calls after me in a pitiful voice:

"Oh, sir."

It would be better if he shouted something harsh, some command. This sick, unnatural plaintiveness is frightening, in an officer of an army of occupation, holding conquered Paris.

"Oh, sir," he repeats, and catches up with me. His eyes are dull.

"Herr Lieutenant?" I say coldly, waiting for him to say whatever it is he has to say.

At first he does not speak, looks at his shoes.

"You are the first person that has come along this street in twenty minutes," he says; "you don't realize that?"

"Odd," I say, "but I hadn't realized."

"Excuse me for interrupting your thoughts," he says.

"Don't mention it," I say between my teeth.

"I am overwrought today. I feel I have to talk to somebody."

"At your service."

"I did not want to conquer your beautiful Paris, believe me," mumbles the officer.

"Indeed no," I mumble back. We can scarcely hear one another.

"My feet are sore from visiting the museums," says the officer after a while. I make no comment.

"I am dog tired from reading titles of books on your old bookstalls, so romantic," he continues, and then adds, "Won't you walk a little? I do not want to keep you from your business."

Then, as we continue along the quay, he says:

"I had always promised myself that on the bookstalls of Paris I would hunt for every single novel of your great artist Romain Rolland. Droll, isn't it, that, being here, and finding all in one fell swoop the entire collection at one bookstall, I should have lost all desire to possess the collection, or even one volume in it! Will you join me in a cigar?"

"I never smoke."

"Neither does the Fuehrer. Discipline, you know. I am not an ascetic myself: I am too gemütlich, I suppose." He spits the bitten black mouthful of leaf he wrenched off the end of his cheap cigar into the street. Then he lights the thing and begins to smoke, still talking sadly, looking over my head at the roofs of the buildings, as if he were searching for some familiar house, some familiar mansard window. (It turns out he isn't, for he has never been in Paris before.)

"You know," he says, "somehow I wish the war were over. Not that I am disloyal. But I love my home. I think of my home."

"Where is your home?" I ask.

"It doesn't matter," he replies. "Only think of a droll little house in a village or dorf: the windows are surrounded with honeysuckle. Inside my father, an old Swedish Hollywood actor, bowlegged and with big artificial eyebrows, bent double from the care and repair of bicycles, is at work. My mother, a fat popeyed old woman who weeps a lot, is waiting for me to return from Paris: I shall come home bringing food, I shall kiss my mother, and she will weep with great big eyes and a little sorrowing mouth. Remember Lew Ayres coming home to his mother in *All Quiet on the Western Front?*"

"I do," I admit.

"I think constantly of that scene. It is part of my life. It is the scene of my own homecoming that will never actually take place. I am so weary," he adds, "from walking around the museums that I could fall down on the sidewalk and go to sleep."

Presently he says, with a little annoyance:

"You are too well bred to question me concerning my real home?"

"Please speak of whatever you wish."

"It is not like the house in the movies. But that is all I dream of. The house in the movies is more really Germany than the real places where I have lived, although I love these in a different way."

He is again silent. Then says:

"Weinachten. Noël. Natale. Funny, isn't it? All those different words mean Christmas. And when I think of Christmas, I think of a jolly German household I once saw in a beautiful film: and Don Ameche dressed as a Tyrolean, rushing in the door."

"You sure saw a lot of movies," I say.

"No more than anybody else," he answers defensively.

Another silence. The expression on his face changes.

"Lew Ayres," he says again, "Lew Ayres goes to this field hospital. Remember?"

"Vaguely."

"Vaguely," he says with great bitterness. "Dear heaven: can't you *see* him trudging along the road with a pair of shiny boots in his hand for his comrade. How he smiles. His comrade will be so happy to get the present. Remember then what happened?"

"No."

"Why, don't you know how he looked at the bedclothes, and where the legs should be, there was nothing? The anguish on his face? The weeping, wounded comrade? You saw the picture, didn't you?"

"Yes."

"All last winter I thought of this. What would I do in a circumstance like that. But none of my comrades has yet lost a leg. Naturally, I've seen some action, though. Who hasn't?"

"Well, what would you do if your comrade had his legs shot off and you had brought him a pair of boots as a present."

"I think I would kill myself," said the officer with tears flooding his eyes.

"No!"

"Perhaps not. Don't think I don't dare kill myself, though."

He broods for a few steps more. I am tired of him and was before I ever met him.

"Do you remember," he says, "the death of Lew Ayres, in *All Quiet?*"

"Yes, that I remember."

"That day gave the title its significance," said the German officer in a dull voice, for he was narrating to me the story of his own death. "All Quiet! Hardly a shot was fired. It was spring. It must have been eerie, in the other war, a day like that. It is warm. Lew Ayres remembers spring, home, woods and villages. Dear Württemberg! Anyway, beauty, in the shape of a butterfly, suddenly appears, innocent and terrible, a miracle of life in the midst of death. I have brooded much about this scene, and the metaphors are my own. It has great significance to me. Lew Ayres, you see him smile, to behold this little, carefree insect. He longs to take it in his hand."

The lieutenant stretches out his hand toward the Seine.

"He climbs up, crawls over the side of the trench, smiling like a child, careful by instinct, and everybody knows what to fear there is a French sharpshooter with a black beard. See how he lifts up his telescopic sights. He doesn't realize. If only someone could convey to him what is in the heart of the German soldier boy, even a Frenchman would soften. If only . . . Oh," cries the officer in unfeigned anguish, "how I longed to be able to stand up in my seat in the theater and cry out in French: 'Ne tirez pas, soldat français! Lew Ayres n'est pas votre ennemi, en ce moment! Non, il attrappe le papillon! Il attrappe le papillon! Ne tirez pas!' But fate and death are inexorable, nothing can be changed: Lew Ayres' hand is almost ready to gently close on the fluttering, winged creature, and oh, the Frenchman's finger tightens on the trigger."

The German lieutenant violently clenches both his hands and turns up his haunted, sad, now tearful eyes, and, jamming his teeth together, lets out a horrible groan, straining all the tendons of his neck upward at the blue sky over captive Paris.

"He dies," groans the lieutenant. "You see the hand, the poor hand of Lew Ayres, fall limp, and lie open, and the tiny, lovely butterfly flutters by, winging away like life itself, out of his grasp."

"I remember this extremely touching moment myself," I say quietly, edging away.

The German officer is content to let me leave. He is not going to follow me with his conversation. He merely leans tragically on the bridge and says:

"When I entered Paris with the Fuehrer's victorious regiments (naturally not the first, by any means, for I have only been here two months), I remembered that little butterfly. I thought then that Paris ought to have been leveled to the earth, but I really don't care. Besides, it was only a film."

"Yes," I say, "quite true, quite true. Adieu, Herr Lieutenant."

And he, leaning on the rail of the bridge, says, in a tone of utter disgust, "Farewell."

XXIII

JOURNAL: PARIS

I am known in Paris as a writer, but only to the police. Strange, isn't it? Before my questioning by whoever the officer was, I used to think, Perhaps my journals will be brought out in the courtroom and read, and I will explain them as best I can, without affectation, pretenses, translations, or fear, and the whole thing will get read into the record of the court, and in this way my journals will have been, accidentally, published.

That did not happen, and I am not crying about it.

Today: supposing I am under the big fake arches of a theater and look through the thin wall of the footlights at a dimly shining garden of shaved heads? Suppose that, standing at the top of a podium, I nod and bow and wonder over the vastness of a big aquarium of half-sights, settling semi-sounds, and rustle my papers at the inceptions of complete order made before me by a vast pseudo-literary guild of occupying Schutzstaffel policers.

With what meekness, what timid sharpness, the preliminary cough: with what urbanity make I the first four words, and pause and hear the clear calm voice of the explainer go flying around the theater to the perhaps curious. It is

a public lecture on the subject of literature and the arts: I
open:

"Bigge Gude Dog-wife, says Shag-spur, muggy wuggy
smug Dutch: and, elsewhere in *Hamlet,* from which I
wrench my text, Double your smackspits if you would
goggle your vulgar apprehension toward this evening's re-
frainment, Bobby Dutches. Sit up! Beg! Wag! Plague dead,
Towsbottom! Ease up your big armpits, you jiggy-dog tooth-
wifes from Strumbury, let out your gurse, settle your oaky
legs, remove your mechanical heads, and listen to the ras-
senfragels lipspeech of Mr. Lettercatcher.

"Dames is always a bug for lettercatcher. Novels is neat
and smart. Novels is got five parts: the copy (publishes it
the Big Jugurtha Publishing Business. Ten cents), the cover
(picture of some steam), the part you sit in (or armchairs
as big as a bed), the part you knock out your pipes on
(Molly Kisses Huggy Gue), and the end (viz. the honey-
culture modicums of Raccknowledge which we conclude
from what we waded through). Sick Heil! Stand up and
bow. Sit down and button your buttons. Now breathe a bit
and stop coughing and I will pursue.

"In case you bobs imagine you are the more or less unique
germings in the roost which my speaks is aimed at, let me
allow myself to permit the following definition of Dutch:
'Anybody who likes to eat live meat, irrespective of his
original race creed or belief.' That includes Mucky Harry
sitting by the bridge of London's sobstruck Thames, no
closer than Harpy Carlo leaning on the towers of Pusha or
growling in the empty glades of Brandenburg, without
benefit of clergy. I pretend to include a big sweep with
what I aver, and I may talk frontwards and aim backwards,
and assume I am looking east and west if you can imagine
nothing less so to save your lives, seeing the four-cent
state of your usual fantasies.

"Wipe your wives and brush your food out of your face

and make like you understand words, and sleep in the glory of my following speech, which is in no manner daunted with interludes of frisky defining, you bloody great loaves of stone.

"I will condemn my treatment of the nobbil with my holdup and slaughter of the Grigs Eppig. Dames is crazy for Grigs Eppig. Eppig is a Thursday poem cut to the length of the Sunday's paper and not to be funned without the mauls of the digsyournary. But dames grab every page with their teeth and chew it slow and noisy like a cow in a field of paper grass.

"What do you get from the Grigs Eppig? All stuffed up with paper until you are bearded and dull and can't walk backwards nor floorwards with your huge encumberments of expensive amusement gone to waste. Sit down, sit down, sir! Down! (Whip him, somebody, he's growling for a bone again!)

"Well, supposing somebody give you the Grigs Eppig of some Grig arthur. Quick, get your manuals: whip over the pages and find the entry: Grigs. 'Grigs,' I quote with infinite abandon, 'is a chink-jew conquered race.' Snap shut your books, go back to gnawing your meats for a minute, while I continue to explain, wasting my breath. 'Ef thes es so-o, et follows thet: one the Grigs Eppig is some kind of telephone book written by a jig-nigger. Put it down to the dumps, tear out the first four pages, begin to Page Nine, where it say, Lulu loves the weasels.' Shall we let yer get away with the Man of Laws or remain firm to the Paris? (not to be confused with the part of space where we are now suffering from this interlude of intellectual chess, since this is the name of one of the chinks in the boog).

"I need go no further. Is not this amazing smart for a book writ by greekjap jigaboy barbario-rassenbodies no less than a hundred years ago by my computation? Of course it is. Thank you for your applause.

"(Attendant, hit that man with your club, will you, he is biting all the others and creating a stir. Down, down, sir! Do you want to be deprived of your dog meat, or will you be civil?)

"But in sum, if I somerset myself backwards in a white circle of dazzling agility and land upwards on my feet back where I started in the deeper muds of your more sluggish comprehension, to which I am paid poor money to condescend, open your big mouth and catch the following simile if you are capable. It is poetic, a little, but you shouldn't mind, for so are you, at least in your own minds:

"Big Gug Spatface is handsome without teeth. He is our hero, just as much in New York as in Frankfort on the Oder. Sputface ducks food, thrown by Harry Breath, his lunatic neighbor, the gauleiter of Leeds. What do you suppose occasioned their doggy wrastle, their heavybody kickinthemiddle jujitsu as subtle as mashing with hammers? It is a difference that claims to be immortalized in the works of lettercatcher. Letters will make you all heroes, you big lumpy stupid barking hurdy-gurdies! Lay down and scratch, then, or I will have you tied up for a week. The comparaison I meant to compare is something like a metaphor, as if that could mean anything to a grand old Smut like you.

"The best literature is trimmed like a mustache and marches to parties and oppresses all the women with dogma concerning the race. But what we swear we like to read (eh, sly snarlers all, leafing over the flesh of your kill) is more like the Beowulf comics or the Giant Feelies, or the *Chewy Cripple Book,* or the *Monster Passion Stories,* or *Thirdbase Dementia,* or *Mouth Delerium,* or *Pulpy Detective,* or *Kissy Whiplaughter Flesh Stories.* This is the best literature because it adorns a moral by means of action and points an effect in relation to a cause; for example, clear as broken bones comes this message from the poets:

"Gob my glud, Feely Shirley, hissed Paul, smack me the

dance halls in the middle of the puss if I don't swelter for youse with the crudest sensations of sweat. I am the honest-est groat smig duggle football you'll ever play, you red mouth you, so get on your chewies and we'll smashbash the car into Flegmy's Seven Corners to fool the police and what we won't do in the gasoline I leave you to imagine by butting your head against the bars of the jail where you crumpled the warder with a iron pipe. Sledge my beat, swamp my crummy beastfat ideas if this ain't honest realism. Slough him in the tooth, sweetie, break him with a house, and mouth him up with your gobby speeches of face be-fore the entranced can fall through the bags of literature you have accumulated here and expire in wonder at their portraits, portrayed no less than by a foggograph of suds.'

"This was a classic from *Breedy Foulies,* by none less than Harper Herpingway. So shut up and listen while my words beat against the thick fibers of your ears with the sound of a drum. Clap shut your teeth for an instant. Stop popping out your brass eyes, for the clangor is too tremendous in here. I shall have to ask the attendant to remove that person who is killing Albert with the chair, unless he will give an absolute guarantee, signed in the thick white invisible ink of his own blood, that he will sit down and whimper like the rest of them.

"Up smugs, race your ears after this stick of dry clot:

"'What is Rassengedicht? Ballads say our race is two times heavier than the chink-jap sneakies trying to whittle the edges of our empire. Our poems is got more albumen in it than theirs, and is cross-eyed with more rage. When we read our Gedicht, it clatters like a coin telephone receiving a quarter, whereas theirs is not the same, but in an in-ferior forging language, probably Russ. Where's the fever in their white words? Gow blobs, I spit weasels to hear the works of Goiter, not less Frowst than Schilligs Roiper, not less this than Mugscrew Yawnold's Dover Speech, and

Lawsy Byron's imitations by Whistler's mother: Chet Long-
fellow.'"

Every man Jack will sit up and step when racy letters
hath so much zip. Yay, griggy, pass me the Song of the
Shirt, it has a sociable theme, and I'm crazy for a jolt according to tomorrow's party line. Get your informational
biographies, Jobber, and it will put sleds in your pencil,
and you will certainly get promoted from a thief to a mur-
derer when you eat them popular best salads of the month:
Look Boneward Beagle and the best of the bunch, *Mine
Strife*, by (leap up and spit and crack your arms at domes of
the roof) Unser Fog-Dog Jiggyboy Leapfrog Aunt Alfred
Hitler, the hope of the Razzle frage and the favorite act in
Oscar Spengler's *Nightlife of the Nineteenth Century*, OUR
CHAMP!

"(Speak Heil, Speak Heil, Speak Heil.)"

And at this mention of the champion nonfiction seller of
the age all the frowzy heavyweights throw down their wives
and the soups they were drinking furiously and yowl like
the tempests of Valhalla, and the whole dumb place rocks
like it was undermined with Wurlitzer organs, because
their candidate is the big money-maker of the whole field
of modern letters, and if I seem to laugh when I am saying
that, I partly laugh on the other side of my face, but partly
also smile with some confidence to think that, if Hitler is the
most published writer of this age, I, as it turns out, am the
least. Maybe the conclusions I draw from this are a source
of dangerous pride, and yet I hope that there is something
in it. I sure do.

But meanwhile, they are firing their arms into the air
like javelins every two seconds and piercing the roar of
seventy-seven bands with the knives of their yells, and I
climb down from the stage, which is being taken over by
a team of acrobats, and retire in a brown study to my al-

bergo, or, in other words, to the quiet and sad reality of the summery river Seine, that sorry fleuve!

There is no wind in the leaves of the trees. I walk without sentiment, along the quay, looking at the green water. O Seine, I never saw the canotiers with their red mustaches and their girls dappled with light; I never saw the blue sky at Argenteuil, nor Seurat's speckled picnic. Where are all those people gone, with their tight collars, and their speech as precise and angry as their coats/ Where are their trussed up women that sat, all collared and serious, among the green grasses/ Where are the cyclists and the rugby players of long ago, who flashed through the trees as solemn as Douanier Rousseau, passing the ball but both passer and receiver looking straight ahead, and the ball hung abstractly between them/ I never saw this river in those suburbs, because I had not yet been born.

The streets used to be filled with people who knew just what they were doing, who cared about the way they kept their hats and shoes and umbrellas, who believed in their furniture, who knew where everything in Paris was, who knew where to look for the people they knew. They were surprised at colds in the head, they were irritated by a remark about music, they gave no thought to the gaslight globes in the dance halls and cafés, and yet were critical of the lighting in the picture galleries. Everything was crowded, everywhere. But everybody had a seat in the imperfect but familiar theaters, and the noisy cafés. All the while, Proust was in his room writing, and the world was firmly established.

Nobody wondered what was important, because everybody knew. The poor knew that their respectable squalor was important, the rich that their respectable inertia was important. The wheels of the carriages flickered in the streets like the shimmering of water in the sun. The lungs of the cyclists filled with the smoke and spring of the velodromes. The oarsmen's girls sang faintly and shyly on the sunny river, where the railway bridges clattered like nickelodeons under the trains de Banlieue.

The skinny shadows of symbolist poets, converts to Catholicism, linger in the absinthian green of the Boulevard trees. Under their hats, their pale eyes shine like tea, and their skins are thin as blue-white buttermilk. The dumb stone figures in Père Lachaise stand openmouthed as if to utter republican or even communist hymns. The frowning abattoirs and warehouses of Montparnasse encourage the ball-playing children to cry out like sparrows in the darkness of their shadows.

Somewhere in the infinity of all these crowds is a place for the articulate, profane apocalypse of Léon Bloy, which is apart from the crowds themselves and is only now beginning to be fulfilled, in their death, in this huge silence.

But now the trees roar over my head like a crowd in a theater. The quay trembles with the terrible applause of a passing bus (see the German soldier reading his army newspaper on the rear platform).

In and out the arcades under the Comédie Française walk, slowly, the huge impresarios, surrounded by saluting soldiers. The virtuosi are immense and walk as though they were half blind and had to feel their way with canes. The bulbs of the uniformed reporters flash under the arches, tiny French politicians run forward, holding their hats and gloves. The whole thing is an elaborately contrived insult: the production, in German, of *Egmont,* by, of, and for the conquerors, on the stage of the Comédie Française. Where are the hundreds of Middle Western American schoolteachers who used to sit in here, in tears of boredom at Le Cid? They are replaced by perplexed German soldiers, by illdressed men of the Gestapo, ready to sit with their arms folded watching the entrances and exits of the building for three hours.

The soldiers enter the theater, blushing to the backs of their necks, not knowing whether it is a leader's funeral, or a speech by the Fuehrer, or what it is going to be, that they have been summoned there to sit through.

The men of the Gestapo hesitate in crude embarrassment, in the doorway, each one holding his allotted ticket and wondering whether or not to take off his hat. They crowd into the darkness inside. Four French children cross the square, looking away from the theater. More buses full of German soldiers come thundering to the doors. The children disappear into a side street. The cattle clatter of feet and the presence of many awed, breathing creatures fills the arcade, where the speechless soldiers fall instinctively into line.

In all the empty streets rings the voice of the radio commentator:

"Caro populi inferior.

"Rouse. Weck. Sturz. Bekom. Gross lettercatchers is the orders of the day. Guess you no comprenny, you jigsfrench. Youse of the lapin races, aside, hide in your lascivious newspapers. Faz dolor di honta rossu figuro. Ecartez vous, cheaps. Hoc es fe Trowel-spiel, or the Roarspiegel. Begins in the first with Latin declensions, fur monstrar la natura clásica de la fiesta. Continua mit whole speeches from imitation marble paradigms, eventually concatenating intself upwards into a Durchbruch of the meistens emotive hocking and choking: il y a des scènes dans la rue, et d'autres encore dans la maison. The whole thing plays like an organ, ja, ein grosser Orgel full from batsnests in the pipes thereof. Otra particularidad di isto traggidiu is che the personnages are all called Wolfgang. Take offense, you crafty Gallic chinks, and swear you Mediterranean Smyrnese of Parisis. Questa sera si recita con intenzione di farvi break your dents with gringing and clashing. Meanwhile all the Wolfgangs begin their frays and processioni,

perfectamente Nordicu, auf them Strassbahns, them auto-
matic railways of the stage, and commence rioting in the
airplanes of the scenery until the impresarios jostle one
another into a state of quasi dementia in the wings.

"Udir, con permesso: farvi projettar a platto con su
nombril faceforwards down on the street with admirations
of the following coy sentiments of shirty Wolfgang gagging
in the dungeons of the Dutch.

Wolfgang: "Grobb mein schuttel, will ich nicmands heiss'
     Snob sein spittle schmuck dir Butter neiss?
     Schnavak, Schnavokli, piutro schmiggid gopp
     Weilohne Freiheit, Freedom comes to stop."

People: "Gut big Wolfgang! Blond Haar! Fat tooth!
Wide head! One of us! Zeitgenossen! Make him our Eagle
from Wednesday to Sunday; he is so crafty and dumb we
will follow him into the cistern!"

Wolfgang: "Schreck makken Schrecklich, Zitter ja vor Zeur!
    My massive clapper-Zahne smatchen
     furious by the hour!
    Zeriss', Zeriss', the render is gekomm'
    To crack your Charlies like a chikken-boon
    And beate out Harry's ribben for their
     marrow
    And Jaws zerissen simply fur den horror.
    Geschreck, geschrack! The Rassenfrag'
    Gelosen ist mit viclen Tranen for youse
     French tomorrow!"

People: "Hear Albert sprecht! Weisheit! Sapianz, smart
as a door, heavy as a false leg, powerful as an engine,
merciful as a slate roof, credible as a victrola, comprehensible as a column of logarithms, settled as a stomach, friendly
as a garage, honest as a pocketful of pawn tickets, and
happy as a suitcase in an attic. Hochzeit! You have married
our minds with your tragical sneaks of rodderick. Precip-

itate yourself into a half-dozen more murders and we are your little cousin Baldur!"

Wolfgang: Geblitz! Rowse myth them Franzose! Ik gesag'
        Mattina rennt Italieni auf lo stesso Jagd!
        Pinzer Panzer, snip your pinchers, liess
            te flammenwerfer los
        Herren Damen in the Beispiels where
            they gone nobody knows.

People: "Soldaten figur! Herrlich! Nice use of the word Beispiel. Aplatis toi, Gallicu meandro. Me and my business associates have sworn on the empty safe to be true to Lieutenant Narcissus the Aryan midget, big as a tack and brainy as an electric current, jumpy as a bean and the world's most prominent author. Go feed on the heartbroken sentiments of your French flesh from this day forth. Your myths have been superseded. Your lunches have already been devoured in anticipation by the cross-eyed babies of the Gestapo's beaten haggards, so let the curtains come swishing inwards in the middle of the last line, and warn the world our classic rage has simmered down to a little point, a kind of snuffing. I thank, soldaten. Wipe up the band, and all sing our love songs: 'When Judy's blood will on the dagger striltz!'"

(With these words the curtain falls with a crash, as if the ropes had all been cut, and the play is at an end.)

XXIV

Most of the public clocks in the city, except certain ones looked after with particular care by the army of occupation, have stopped. The clocks in the hotel are all dead. The calendars, in most places, are unchanged. Besides, since I never read the papers or carry a watch of my own, I would scarcely know how to locate myself in time at all if it were not for my missal, which I follow from day to day, and for the bells of a convent locked among the houses somewhere behind my hotel.

I wonder about the convent: I can see the little belfry from my window, among some squalid roofs. But, walking around the streets, I can nowhere identify any building as having the face or character of a convent. It is probably entered through one of the houses and is located behind them all, walled in and isolated from the city. (I think of the secret convent in Puebla, in Mexico, entered through tunnels from a dull-looking bourgeois living room.)

Now I think of secret convents: of rooms with clocks shining under glass bells, with Dresden china vases on the mantelpiece, with a fading, brown, egg-shaped photograph of a man in sideburns hanging on each of the four walls;

of upright pianos heavy with small souvenirs of Aix les Bains, Lausanne, Dinard, Quimper, Fontainebleau lined up on top: I mean china pigs, china wooden shoes, china everything, hundreds of tiny, meaningless, breakable objects. But you only have to move the piano and there is a secret passageway. A draft from the hidden convent stirs the curtain.

Few sounds come from there: not the thin voices that sing the Little Office, not the sound of washing dishes. All is silent. I praise the little nuns in the secret convent in my imagination. Peaceable, serious, undramatic, they sit in a circle, sewing, and not talking nonsense, and, in fact, not talking at all. I praise them; there is no nonsense in their house. All nonsense has been locked out by a secret passage blocked, at the other end, by an upright piano. I do not know who has begged, for them, their food. I do not know what simple, useful things they sew in love and thoughtfulness, making much peace in a small, dull, ugly room where there is no ornament except perhaps the most commonplace and least aesthetic of religious pictures. I do not know their different religious names. I do not know what priest brings in to them, smuggled, the Body of Christ.

Here is nothing exquisite or dramatic, not in the room: yet supposing this is in a country where the convents are illegal, then, if they are caught, perhaps the nuns will be put in prison or shot for liking to live in a room and sew and pray and turn sadly away from nonsense. The only drama is that they may be compelled to come out and either talk nonsense and vulgarity or be punished. Until then they touch no money, think nothing theatrical, frame in their minds no argument to anybody's hurt, and do not even make up, in their thoughts, any haggling answers to the gangster who may someday judge and insult them, because they think absolutely no nonsense at all. My imagination praises them, wherever they are, for their childish and careful prayers are part of my life: the prayers in secret of the nuns, for the world, are part of God's love, whereby I am able to live.

Meanwhile, what is going on in the world outside?

The world outside is filled, by accident, with some strange lost voice that cries, in cultivated English:

"Wanda, where are you, can you hear me? Where are you?" I do not know where this fantastic voice is coming from, and how it comes to have been picked up by all the radios in Paris, instead of the usual propaganda. Can this be something the Germans are using? The voice cries, again, with the unmistakable accents of serious, suffering stupidity:

"Wanda, can you hear me? Where are you?"

Just that. It is repeated over and over. It is unutterably pathetic, that voice. Then suddenly, there is an answer. A sharp and business-like woman's voice, clear as water, quite cold, but not calm.

The woman's voice says:

"All right now. Are coming through now. Go ahead."

I feel like Coleridge's Ancient Mariner lying in the redwhite shivering heat where is entranced his ship of zombies, while ringing in the metal air over my head are these quiet disembodied voices, right next to one another, yet at a great distance from one another, exchanging the confidences of spies or saboteurs. I am terrified and fascinated by the voices that trade their sharp, unintelligible, impersonal words, that begin to sound like anything at all, like prophecies, like omens, like incantations.

"Banks of Yarrow (do you hear me?), Banks of Yarrow will be all snapdragons. The traveler will come to the columbines. Four-four in the threshold of the waning year Sylvanus (do you follow me?) faintly drums. Then the waders triumph in the hay, and the watchers sleep in the tower."

There is silence, as if the air were suddenly dead of voices, but the voices are still there. The woman's says sharply:

"Right. Continue."

The other voice continues, monotonous, without any variations of pitch or emphasis, except unnatural ones:

"When the gate is dark (have you this?): when the gate is dark, two-two in the threshold of the rising moon Sylvanus plays the lute-string river. The sea is crowded with the noise of clocks. But the windows of the city flower, after a long darkness, like marigolds. The watchers in the tower are alert, but the travelers, sleeping in the columbines, smile. Repeat four-o-six twice. Begin with Sylvanus and retell in two-two, alternating the words of the flowers. Delphia is cornflower, Paphos a tiger lily. Now continue."

"Okay," says the woman's voice after a second.

"When the tower is lost, and the rose in the dust lies dead, and the traveler is arising from among the milkweeds with dew upon his eyes, then the world rusts like a forsaken instrument and the cry of the water wheels becomes harsh. There is no one in the gate. Trees talk like hinges when the wind begins. Sylvanus is as starving as the panes of windows. Destruction looks out of the casements because tomorrow is the ending of the world. That is all."

"It fits," says the woman's voice. "Switch over."

"Right," says the man's voice sadly, "begin."

"Ecclesiastical sonnets are now being offered regularly in the Hotel of the Ambassadors, where ruin comes geranium red. There is nothing further to be expected from the corridors of the sun. Sylvanus shines in the windows of the harvest evening like a coin. Twenty-one hundred is the day of the regret. The portals of the waning years are becoming apocalyptical doors. The tulips are alone in lamenting the scarcity of rain. The shepherds will prepare to make for Mount Ida in a boat. The windows of the city, opening like mouths, on their departure, will swear in the terrible drought like swarming locusts. The water wells are forgotten, and the suffering of the thirsty wounded echoes in the barrels of the gate like the anger of guitars. Sylvanus will take everything and leave by the west; Comus will lead off to the southeast. The wind, playing in the empty towers, shall slay all others with the shivering of the bugle. You and I meet two miles west by north of the crossroad in the valley of Joshaphat. Tell Comus and Sylvanus to be there before compline: that is the last evening before the first morning. Toll all our men to be there. Compline is the end of the regular day, forever. Do not sing your word too late. Now we are beginning to be ready in the watchtowers, because the wells are nearly dry. That is all the water we have left. That is all."

"Okay," says the man's voice, "switch over."

"Ready."

"This is short. The holidays will run like the sound of horses under the house."

"Is that all?"

"Yes, that is all."

And the air is silent. The voices have disappeared.

Immediately I go downstairs and out into the street. Walking out of the hotel is like walking out of a movie. The street is real, familiar, and hard on the eyes. I walk drunkenly a few steps down the sidewalk and am stopped by a French soldier.

It is my friend the interpreter, who argued for me in the court the other day.

"Eh bien, bonjour, poète!"

"Que tal, soldado."

"Why are you sad?"

"I am disturbed by what is in the air, everywhere. The radio in the next room to mine picked up some British propaganda about the end of the world. It was mysterious, lyrical, and a little frightening."

"If it impressed your imagination, it was probably not British propaganda, then," says the soldier. "Tell me what was in it, and I will tell you whether or not it was British? Was it Christmas carols, rugby players, Tewkesbury Abbey, Stoke Poges churchyard, blond, white-eyed airmen with their mouths all making at once some brave, prim melancholy song? Was it concrete playgrounds, old busted dames made out of steam and brick standing in the ruins like sheep dogs with their hair in their eyes? Was it a religious man with a big Adam's apple and a bitter mouthful of bird speech? Was it a dangerous gang of schoolgirl hockey players, or a village choir standing under the Lych Gate in the shape of a V, for victory? If the talk began with the words 'Our determination is as strong as our tea . . .' and ended with the words "Our resolve is as round as a football,' then it was British propaganda. But if it made you feel sorry for England, and if it made your heart jump silently, inside its place of hiding, then it wasn't British propaganda. Because if you are a poet, the British propaganda makes you sympathize with Germany, and only the German propaganda makes it impossible for you to really like or trust the Germans, throwing you back, once again, upon the British."

I walk, with this soldier, along the street toward the river. At first we walk, saying nothing, but I know what it is the soldier is going to ask me. He says:

"The cops who have invaded us, you know who: they are very stupid, but their stupidity is also terribly thorough. It is harder to escape them than it is for a figure to get out of place in an addition made by a machine: then how did you get into France?"

I laugh. "By accident, I suppose."

"I will not ask you to tell me how, of course," says the

soldier. "You may as well know I am paid by the Gestapo, anyway. Not to follow you, or anything like that, merely to bring in miscellaneous information."

"If they don't arrest me for writing what I like, I don't fear them."

"Oh, they'll let you alone, more or less, from now on," says the soldier, "unless they find out you got through them, into France, and that you aren't supposed to be here. I don't think they'll find out now, though."

Then he says:

"But why did you come back? To write about it? Uncensored reports?"

"In a sense, except that I have already been censored. The censor didn't understand what he read, and so didn't touch any of it. Would you call that uncensored?"

"I suppose it is. I hope it isn't like all the other uncensored stuff, which is so dull that it might just as well have been censored to pieces, for all the information it contains."

"It is different from that, I hope," I say.

"But what," says the soldier, "did you come back to see?"

"I cannot think, now," I reply. "But perhaps it was the place where the long black Paris train used to wait in the rain at Boulogne harbor, stretching far out of the station among the labyrinthine streets of the dockyard section."

"That has been terribly bombed, I imagine," says the soldier, "that, and the houses all up the side of the hill, and the church on top of it. I may be wrong."

"The train still seems to be standing along the track outside the station. The cars, marked 'Nord,' are France; the Wagon-restaurant does not smell of tea, but of food. The corridors of the train make the English uneasy with their raw smell. In the compartments of the train, the tawdry, much-handled copies of the *Daily Mail* look ill at ease, and English has, at last, become a foreign language again."

"What else did you come back to see?"

"Perhaps the big square at Dijon, where in the late light of the evening of Bastille Day, the soldiers come riding in their shining plumed helmets across the cobblestones, and the tall, delicate houses heard everywhere the shrillness of the lovely fanfare coming from the streets hung with strings of colored bulbs.

"My father and my brother and I stand in the crowd, and the plumes nod. The manes of the horses toss with the excitement of the bugles. Beyond the heads of the people, the dark green trees make dance their stately masses in the light summer wind. I believe the soldiers pass through a triumphal arch all strung with electric lights, but I do not remember if we ever saw the display of fireworks.

"Dijon, you sing to me in the nights of summer like the fifes of my ten years' age, and your dusk is all entranced with lights, like strings of beads!

"We are in a music store, not far from the cathedral: the doorway opens on to the narrow street (where the lights are strung, and not yet lit, for this is before the parade). The small store is dark and is filled with the brown, shining, and angular shapes of the upright pianos.

"I stand in the front of the shop, hearing the quiet footsteps of the people in the street outside, smelling the smell of new sheet music, looking at the window full of ocarinas, harmonicas, flageolets and little flutes, and a violin in an open case. Behind me, in the store, where my little brother stands among the pianos without fuss, my father begins to play some tune, sitting seriously on the piano stool, with his pipe laid on the end of the keyboard, where he will forget it (and he never gets it back). The tune is called 'Chicago,' or 'Tea for Two,' or 'I want to be happy, but I can't be happy, till I make you happy to-o.'

"The people of Dijon walk by the window. They can't see, from the summer street, back into the darkness of the store where my father plays 'Chica-go that ci-ty of brotherly love, brotherly love.'

"My grandfather and grandmother sit in front of the white tablecloth in the high-ceilinged dining room of the hotel, waiting for us to come back. But we are far off in the town, in which they are not interested. They perch at the dinner table in the hotel like people in a far, fortified tower aloof from the world. We are in the music store, playing 'Tea for two, me for you, you for me, two for tea, tea for you, tea for me, me for you, you for me, tea for two, how happy we will be-e-e.'

"O Dijon, all the windows in your high, clear houses have the expression of France. The arched windows of the churches, rising light and rare and brave as dancers, say, 'France.' The late light of the sky makes glad the colored geometric designs in the slate roofs of the city, and everywhere the lights shine, the imitation jewels of the nineteenth century glittering among the medieval houses, and nothing is in conflict, but everything is at peace in the clean, serene town, Dijon!

"My father and my brother and I come walking home through your streets, to the hotel. The high mansards of the hotel flash with the red reflection of the sun, late-setting on the hills full of vines. The cobbles are ready for the iron clatter of hoofs, and the walls expect the brass excitement of the trumpets, but in the silence before the drums begin, the whole city sings in the evening sky like a clean hymn. The churches are not old; they are young. The medieval city is not old, but speaks with the clarity and innocence of childhood. The strings of bulbs, the nineteenth-century arch, the new hotel are older than the old houses, and the helmets of the soldiers, with their Third Empire plumes, will seem incredibly ancient. But the roofs and spires that sing in the summer evening, because the vines are beginning to shine with fruit, are all as young as the vineyards and the sky, and sing in the evening like a hymn."

"These things are what you came to see," says the soldier, as we come to the quais by the river. "But I do not think you'd dare to go back and see them. What else is there?"

"I am not angry that the Rex Cinema, in the Champs Elysées, is now reserved for German soldiers, although it is the place where I saw Marlene Dietrich in *Shanghai Express*. I am not sure whether I would find the Watteau picture of the Pierrot, in the Louvre, but it is one they would not know enough to take away, perhaps."

"How do you know?" says the soldier.

"Because when I was a child, I couldn't understand why my father and his friend, the critic, stood in front of it and talked about it for half an hour, never looking away at anything else. I didn't believe it was possible to talk that long about any picture, let alone this one, which appeared to me to be absurd, because it was a picture of a sad man in a white suit like a clown's suit, standing with his arms straight down at his sides and looking straight out of the picture. To me, it seemed unnatural to paint a picture of such a subject, and if it seemed so to me, a child, it will seem so to the Germans: and they will leave it where it stands. In that place I came back when my father was dead, and understood the picture better. But I don't know if I came back to see pictures, or buildings, or churches."

"The whole of Beauvais was leveled to the earth," says the soldier, "except the cathedral, left intact out of the most purposeful bravado. Daily it is surrounded by German soldiers taking snapshots of it with their various kinds of cameras, from the cheapest to the most expensive. In the evenings, they all write down in their notebooks and diaries all the exact facts concerning the building, its dimensions, its history, and a detailed list of all the statues and carvings inside and out of it, completed finally by select quotations from the most reliable works of reference, praising various aspects of the design and structure of the famous temple."

"If I had wanted to see only the cathedrals, it would not have been necessary for me to return, or at least to return now. But I wanted to see something more than this."

"What?" says the soldier.

"Signs saying 'Lampisterie' flashing by on small stations on the P.L.M., at night, in March. A fat gendarme rolling a cigarette in a third-class compartment on the Midi Railway. The rugby players arriving home on Sunday night, noisy and tired, carrying their little canvas bags and smelling of cognac. The shooting galleries, lit with sick-smelling acetylene flares that blow wildly and angrily in the night wind over the marshes of the Languedoc coast. The pale green paper, wrapping the stacked blocks of chocolat Menier in the groceries, and the orange wrappers around the thinner slabs of chocolat Poulain.

"I have come back to see the red fermented muck of grape left in the streets when the wine press is taken into the house again, in autumn. I have come to see the provincial ladies drinking grenadine syrup and soda water, at the open air tables under the elm trees in the little towns of the South. And I have come back to see the rusty iron crucifix that stood near the Place de la Condamine in St. Antonin, and to see the very young, black-haired priest that taught in the parochial school, walking like fury through the streets in his cassock. To see the green-glass bottles of mineral water on the tables of small provincial hotels, and to read on the labels the names of the diseases they cure. I have come back to see the blue river curving under the bridge, and to hear the paddles of the laundresses echoing under the arch. I have come back to see this quay where we stand, and look across this other river at the long, dark blank wall of the Tuileries, through the trees, and see the men standing by the bank with fishing poles."

"And what do you find?"

"I no longer hear the squawking of the taxis or the high-pitched klaxons of the omnibuses. I no longer see the people in the streets, nor smell the smell of gasoline, newsprint, hair oil, new bread, artichokes. The city has been struck with the silence of prisons, yet continues in the terrible patience of the dangerously ill. That is what I need to understand."

"Understand?" says the soldier. "I ask you to think of the American newspaper reporters who would give thousands of dollars to be able to be standing here where you are, with their notebooks, and with their cameraman lugging a case of plates behind them. Then they would look around imagining they were able to understand why these buildings, which have not been bombed, look as if they had been bombed. Imagining they were able to understand what is seen in Paris today, they would write careful stories, and get into terrible fights with the censors and finally go home and write their uncensored diaries, and in these would have no more to say than they had already said through the censorship, and the reason they have nothing more to say is not that they are concealing the truth, but simply that, since they think they understand everything they see, they report everything they seem to understand. But since they understand nothing (nobody does, yet), their reports are, consequently, nothing. It is too soon to ask to understand the leprosy that is so plainly invisible to the discerning eye along the walls of the hospitals and academies and law courts and even of the churches of this city. It is too soon to ask to understand the gray words of this heavy river, words plainly inaudible to the listening ears of the catatonic poets. It is too soon to ask the stations as empty as summer ballrooms to become intelligible, and to ask how it happens that all the government offices are stripped of their furniture, and all the hotels are populated with wax figures of the onetime great."

"How long have you been here?" I ask the soldier. "Where did you come from?"

"I will try to tell you," he replies, "about the field full of cornflowers, near Chantilly, where I woke up in the morning, lying on my back with the high sun buzzing in my face like a hornet.

"The sun blazed in my eyes like a brass furnace, and I could not remember the place where I was supposed to have been before I found myself in this field. But it was in Tournai that I got the sores in my mouth, and I am certain that I was actually there, because Tournai is where we went in the gray truck, after the gun lurched down sideways into the canal, and stood half drowned, half drunk, broken, in the weeds and water.

"We were tossed about in the truck like pillows when the gray boats (their tanks) swam toward us through the trees; yet we got away.

"Before we saw the cloud of smoke that made all our eyes get red and blind, I had begun to get the sores in my mouth. I could feel their round burning all over my tongue and palate and gums and lips, big sores in the size of various coins. My head filled with heat. When the smoke got in my throat, the sores burned more fiercely than ever. The sores spread to my eyes and ears when the truck spilled us out in the street like a pile of leaping bricks. I fled from Tournai, followed by a cloud of bees, without having seen any of the city. It immediately became impossible for me ever to imagine again that I had been near any town of that name.

"Long before I was in the field with the cornflowers, I came to a canal. I put my head in the water of the canal to cool the red sores over my eyelids and in my nostrils. The water did not quench the mad, bronze bees.

"I saw a man in the woods waving flags in a semaphore signal: I stood up and signaled back, and saw that it was really a tree holding up a live banner of flame. The sky was full of minnows.

"I ran through the green seas of the grass, away from the road. The sores raged behind my ears, and in the hollow of the nape of my neck the fever glared like a hot coal. A cloud of bees, darkening my sight and deafening my hearing, at last totally filled my eyes and prevented me from seeing anything at all.

"The last thing I saw before I woke up in the field at Chantilly was a white house near Béthune breaking up like a piece of crumbly cake.

"When I awoke, I looked at the blinding light of the sun, which roared in the sky like a buzz saw, but I was scarcely able to move in the grass where I lay. I longed for water to wash the sores that burned in the roof of my mouth, and on my gums. On every side of me I could feel the earth begin to shake. Painfully turning my head, I could see, through the polished, waving wires of grass, a house explode like a puffball, and discharge black smoke like a cloud of spores.

"I came crawling on my stomach through grass and gravel. At last, the cool, parquet floors of the picture gallery soothed my ragged hands and my face full of sores.

"When I woke up again I was in an ice-cold, silent room, and everywhere I looked were aisles of shining floor, on which I lay, and walls hung with paintings of thoughtful goddesses in landscapes of brown and formal trees.

"I stood up and began to skate, in the silence, with no sound whatever. I realized I must be dead, and disembodied. Then once again, I returned from this two seconds' illusion to my body full of bees, lying as heavy and bloated as a sack, yet roaring with emptiness. I began to drag myself along the smooth floor. My legs were limp as quilts.

"I got to the window, and raised myself to the sill. I could feel the cold coming in and blowing upon my eyeballs through the crack under the sash. Through the glass, I saw the world was as gray as in winter, saw that some distant smoke was spreading slowly in the sky like a squid's ink darkening the water of the sea with crooked clouds.

"My mouth was still full of sores, and my hands and face felt burned. My eyes were dry and hard as stones, or shells, but the bees had gone. I found myself in a vast icy silence, watching the smoke spread in the watery sky, throughout a tremendous silence.

"Then I began to be afraid; but not, now, of the Stukas. Now I was afraid that I was perhaps the last man left living on the face of the earth.

"I crawled back to the door of the picture gallery, and there the Germans found me, lying on my face crying out, against the steps, unintelligible words, unheard-of names, and numbers.

"In the hospital it was very quiet except for the inaudible speech of two English airmen at the end of the ward, whose talk was like the drip of water, unbearably cheerful. I could not see these men. They both died before I was strong enough to lift my head, and put my arms (which I was astonished to find were not covered with bandages) through the sleeves of the black bathrobe.

"Once I sat up I could see them when they took away the dead. But once I sat up I not only realized that there was no bandage on my head as I had thought, but also no bandage around my chest, no bandages making heavy my legs. Yet I had believed myself to be totally wrapped up in bandages.

"I asked the German doctors, 'Where are my wounds? Where are my burns?'

"They answered, 'You have neither wounds nor burns,' and it was quite true, I had none at all.

"As soon as I discovered this, I was able to get up and walk. I climbed out of the bed, in my bathrobe, and walked past the bed of a man who was silently dying, his face hidden by a white mask.

"I went out into the corridor, which was filled with the bitter smell of wounds and the hard sick stink of ether. The German army doctors came by without noticing me. French orderlies wheeled new men in, shrouded in sheets, but alive, some of them crying out faintly in their throats as they went by, hidden from my sight.

"I walked the length of the corridor, and looked out of the window where there was a white religious statue standing on a pedestal in the middle of a grassless place.

"When I got back to the door of my ward, I realized I must have made a mistake, for all the beds were filled. I went to the next ward: all the beds were placed in an entirely unfamiliar manner, and I could not find any that could possibly have been my own. I went into the third and last ward on that side of the corridor: it had only half the number of beds in it that mine should have had, and there were men sitting in wheel chairs, and once again there was no bed that could possibly have been mine.

"I stopped one of the French orderlies and told him that I could not find my way back to bed: that someone must have stripped it, and remade it, and put a wounded man in it.

"He asked me the number of my bed, and I did not know it. He asked me what ward I was in: I pointed to the first one.

" 'That ward is full, and so are all the others,' he said.

" 'Then what am I to do?'

" 'Wait here.' "

(We have walked some distance along the quays, until, in the lavender light of the misty summer afternoon, the Cité sits in the river like a heavy ship before us.)

The soldier continues.

"I stood in the corridor of the hospital and shivered. Ether, seeping out under all the paper-thin doors, turned to blue metal inside my nostrils.

"I was frozen and drunk with cold, but suddenly I could see through all the walls of the hospital, which became to me like a big aquarium. I could see, everywhere, the handles for turning up and turning down the iron beds in which the dying men lay. There were hundreds of white pans, of metal frames, of light wheels, of operating tables. Men walked under the light in masks, touching things with sharp metallic sounds as they moved. The teeth of the dying soldiers clicked together like knives. The blue, incandescent wires in their eyes dried out and became extinct. They were then removed from the wards, rapidly, leaving nothing behind them in the hospital but a record of a number and a name, and another uniform among the great pile of ragged bloody uniforms, cast aside behind the building, ready to be burned or in some way destroyed, but meanwhile, like every form of garbage around the place, accumulating because there were no horses to drag it away, and nobody could spare petrol for a truck to remove it.

"I stood upon the ether-smelling stones of the corridor. Two German doctors walked by me without speaking, or apparently thinking, a word.

"Then the French orderly appeared at the other end of the hall, and beckoned to me. I followed him into a cold room full of white metal furniture, where, in the middle of a white table, stood a black wine bottle.

"The orderly had a uniform thrown over a chair. He said:

"'Put on this uniform.'

"'The uniform? Why?'

"'Put it on,' said the orderly. 'Get out of here. They haven't any more beds.'

"'Where will I go?'

"'What does that matter? Get into this uniform and clear out. This is no longer any place for you.'

" 'Is the doctor discharging me?'

" 'Don't be a fool. Hurry up. Dress!'

"Before I left, he gave me a drink of wine, and put a couple of cigarettes into my pocket. Then he pushed me out the back door into the place where the pale sunlight played down upon the garbage heap of uniforms of men who had died.

"I got to the main road, and walked two hundred yards like a drunken man, and then sat down in the dusty grass.

"I looked both ways; the road was absolutely empty. It remained so for three hours. I sat there the whole time, as though drugged. Then I got up and made my way back to the hospital and back in through the same door.

" 'You!' said the orderly. 'I thought I told you to get out of this hospital. Now turn around and beat it.'

" 'I'm thirsty,' I said. 'Give me a bottle of wine to take with me.'

" 'Take with you! You ought to have been in Paris by now. Get out on the road, before something bad happens to you. . . .'

" 'I'm thirsty,' I said. 'Give me some wine, then I'll get out.'

" 'Here,' he said. He took a black bottle, three quarters full, out of the white, sterilized closet. 'Now get out!'

" 'Give me some bread,' I said.

" 'Get out, hop it, if you want to live.'

"As I was going out the door, he put a couple more cigarettes into my pocket.

"I went back onto the road, and sat down in the same place. Another two hours passed, and nothing came by, nothing, not even a dog.

"Then I began to hear bees. They were swarming in the flowers behind me, in the branches over my head. Smoke started to pour into my eyes. My mouth was on fire with sores, real sores, not imaginary. I got to my feet and began to run as if all my limbs were detachable from my body. My head was filled now with the sound of the swarm, now with the totally different sound of tearing paper. My heart kept going off like a gun. The bottle fell from my hands and broke in the road, and in an instant the purple wine was sucked into the blotter of that dusty surface, leaving a dry stain. I broke the cigarettes in my hands and scattered the pieces in the air like confetti.

"In a blue octroi booth where an old woman had once sat, I saw the face of a German soldier brooding through the window glass. I stood and watched him until he disappeared. There was really nobody there.

"The grassy ditches of the fortifications of Paris stank of filth. Pieces of newspaper, faded by the rain, lay like dead birds among the grasses. The tall tenements opened their blind sardonic windows on every side, and three German soldiers drove by across the cobbles in a small Citroën, watched from above by the wolfish eyes of old women. Somewhere, where ragged girls were leaning in the window, a tin phonograph began to play some loud and nasal accordion piece, for the benefit of the Germans, who almost immediately disappeared in their car.

"An old woman stood in a doorway as gray as a fish. Her hair fell into her eyes. She scratched her ribs with the hooks of her hands.

"I said:

"'For the love of God give me something to drink, I have crawled here from Chantilly on my face, and I think I am going to die.'

"'Get away from here, or I'll turn you in,' she said. 'Do you think I want to lose my neck for some lousy escaped prisoner?'

"I walked away, toward the wide gap in the fortifications, through which could be seen the wide, resigned faces of the bars and buvettes, standing with torn awnings flapping over their locked doors.

"Thus I re-entered Paris.

"They have left me in peace, here, since I have given them seven or eight pieces of completely fanciful information, and they believe me to be working for them. So, here I am. I don't know why I stay, except that there isn't anywhere else to go. I cannot be sure whether I am waiting for something, because there isn't anything to wait for. I know where I can get bread and soup, and I am sleeping in what is supposed to be my home.

"I might as well be dead," says the soldier, "but it just happens that I am not."

XXV

JOURNAL: PARIS

As I come to the head of the stairs I am aware that my room is open, and that someone is there. I hear the dry bickering of a radio voice coming from the level of my floor: a portable radio is standing in the middle of the room, talking madly to itself.

The stranger is a nervous, bald American in a gray flannel suit. He needs a shave, on his pink American face. He has a large red mustache. He holds out his hand to me, saying:

"I am R., the correspondent for all the newspapers, and the commentator for all the broadcasting companies. I am leaving France today, forever."

I can hardly hear him for the racket of the voice on the radio, which is making its rapid syllables next to his leg:

(Rutcha, Rutcha, grabak! Defaite, neun tausend sechs hunderdt vier und zwanzig, todt, starck positiv, unser, viktoria, sieg, sieg; vorwaerts, vorwaerts, vorwaerts und immer forfeits no more than two or three here and there. Throw your arms out of joint again this morning with a grandiose salute for our eternal victories, and crack your back up straight like a steel flagpole to expect the hourly Heruntergang of treacherous Rutcha. Acht, Neun, Zehn: spit! Vorwaerts! Russland sei verflucht! Learn to sift the dichtung from the Wahrheit in our Neuste Nachrichten: ten thousand million is this morning's lucky number of killed in the huge gross bingo in the east: next week it will all be in the movies. Meanwhile, immer vorwaerts!)

I do not answer the stranger, I cannot think what to say, I shake his hand, which is hot and wet. He repeats:

"I am R., the correspondent for all the newspapers, and . . ."

I nod.

The radio continues imperturbably:

(piggen, zehn millionen: houses destruidos a fondo di comblo: hundred Unserfootstankstroops conquiston hieri die cidade von Pisgah or Kasbah, it isn't clear which: razed to the ground. Seventy-seven million dead . . .)

The stranger wipes his forehead with the back of his hand and says once more:

"And I am leaving France."

"Why have you come to see me?"

He hesitates. He looks at me, diffidently, wondering how I am going to take his next statement. He asks cautiously:

"And you, are you leaving, or are you staying, may I ask?"

"I have no plans. My plans change from day to day. I may leave, I may stay. I am finishing the first volume of my series of journals."

"I knew you were writing a book. That is one reason why I came."

"How did you find that out?"

"The word has gone around. All the censors know about your book." He hesitates, like one who feels that he has committed himself and said too much. I reassure him, or try to:

"I already talked to the censor. He sees no objection to the book I am writing because it is purely personal and has little or nothing to do with politics. Besides, he doesn't understand it."

(Morto cento millieri, massacrado hunderdt von hundert, brennen und arsoniert villaggio après villaggio, destruction general di un caracter formivalento, universali ruinimiento desastros! Horror! Schreck! Such pitiless mighty devastation of vercluchtet Bolschewismus!) So says the radio!

R., after pausing, as though ashamed to be forced to tell me something I ought to have known all along, says:

"Don't underestimate the censors, they are fiendishly clever. I am telling you for your own good, they know all about your salacious memoirs, they know what every word of them means. They have worked out your code by mathematical formulas, and they have a perfect translation in the Palais de Justice right now."

"But it is not written in any code that can be worked out mathematically."

Very embarrassed, but with increasing vehemence, R. says:

"No, no, you are mistaken. I did not mean to tell you all this, because I have reasons for wanting you to stay behind, and this may only scare you away, with me, but I tell you they know what every word of your book means, and they are going to let you finish it, and then make use of it, or you, as they see fit."

"Make use of it?"

"Plainly," says the stranger with some warmth, "the chief censor knows you are writing a pornographic diary. When you have finished it, it will be stolen from you, and that will be the last you will see of your book. Maybe they will print and distribute it surreptitiously among the public that reads such books in all parts of Europe, while, perhaps, burning a few copies in public and sending you to Dachau. Then again maybe they will let you yourself alone. In any case, that is the story which I didn't mean to tell you."

(La escena Rusa makes un paysage molto impresionante, hoy día: approaching in our panzers from dandy leagues away, may be seen and enjoyed the table-flat horizon of the plains where, in the distance, the smokes of burning towns rise into the sky: and the plain looks like the North Sea with a battle fleet under full steam just below the horizon. This remarkably aesthetic effect is of an almost insupportable grandeur when the deep throbbing organ notes of the Fluftwaffle send a tremendous shudder through the earth and sky, in their ceaseless va et vient over the immense battle even now convolving the two greatest and most expensive juggernauts of the earth.)

"Why," I say, "did you not want to tell me this? I am curious to know what you are thinking of, although I am sure your warning is wrong."

"You do not seem to share my suspicions," says R. "Well and good. You do not know these Nazis as I do. Confidentially, they have the cleverness of typewriters and the persistence of adding machines. They are astonishing, they are wonderful, and they are frightful. They are heroic to the point of inhumanity and inhuman to the point of being incredible. They go into battle like algebraic symbols, and they fall and rise like ants. You cannot help admiring them, while detesting, of course, their inhumanity. Please do not use these extremely private and original words of mine, as I am saving them up for my uncensored book which I have been writing with stubs of pencils on onionskin paper now concealed about my person, pinned to my underclothes and to the lining of my suit."

"I do not understand them as well as you seem to, nor respect them as much as you seem to, nor fear them as much as you say you do."

"My dear friend, I assure you, if you were able to foresee what my combined reason and experience and inside knowledge tell me is going to come about, you would not stay in this city another minute. As a matter of fact, before I tell you what I came here to say, I will give you ample warning and urge you to get out. Come with me; I will do what I never intended: give you a chance to come with me. I can get you out of here. I can get you on the clipper, too. I'll give you a chance, although I never meant to."

(Nicht nur in the daytimes but auch in the nighttimes makes the burning of houses a glitter like the distant camps of Tartars and makes shudder the hair-risen imagination with scenes from the Nibelungen forges of the tough dwarf smiths, or perhaps the burning of Troy, far outdone in this the most remarkably romantic and stirring and athletic and thrilling of campaigns!)

He stands there with the helpless expression of a person who is trying, without enthusiasm, to argue me into going to a baseball game. He means what he says about the Nazis, but what he means I do not quite grasp. And he still would like me to refuse. I say:

"I have not finished the work I came here to do. Besides, I am not trying to escape from the same kind of Nazis you are, exactly. I do not think it necessary for me to leave: thank you: go without me. I shall stay a little longer."

Seeing that I am probably set in my refusal, he now says more vehemently:

"You do not know what you are doing. This may be your last chance! Besides, I thought you said you had finished your book? Why stay, then?"

"I have only finished the first of a series."

"Get it out of the hands of the Nazis, or you are lost."

(Que terror muss stricken in the herzen from the Ruschick stupefied paysans seeing our million-million death bird bomber squadrons coming, knife-pointed, horned with wings and sharp shouts, and sowing eggs all over the air as precise as deafening bugs! This is the Aesthetik from kriegs, to see the beauty with which the released bomb sticks flip out of

the planes like fish, and drop at once into straightness and
slide down sideways out of the line of flights: O glorious
beauty, where the city springs up all yellow and gray and
black with smokes like mushrooms! Delizios! Extraordinario!
Delire di refinamiento! Extasis di folor artistique! Caramba,
Russland is attacked like a polyp of darkness by the Siegfried spears of Dutchy's light! Some opera! I can't conceive
it without a big blubber of tears flooding my animal face!)

I cross the room, and open my suitcase, and take the pages
of the journal in my hand:

"This is the book," I say, "the part that is finished."

"So," says R., "even though you have finished that much,
you will not come with me?"

"I think not."

I take the book, and clamp it into a binder, and stick a
blue-framed label on the front, bearing the title and my
name. I hold the volume in my hand, and feel its heft, and
smell the fresh paper and the faint scent of inked typewriter
ribbon; the weight and newness of the finished manuscript
make me happy, in spite of everything this stranger is saying. Here is a book, finished, the first of, I hope, a series.

"Then," says R., coming bluntly to the point, "if you mean
to stay, will you take over my job?"

He wants me to be correspondent for all the newspapers
and commentator for all the broadcasting companies! He
must be crazy.

I say, "I do not write your way."

"You could at least try," he says persuasively. "It is easy
to learn."

"I don't want to learn to write that way. That kind of
writing only makes me feel silly, and ashamed of myself."

"But what will happen if you don't send us news? They
will get nothing but German news, then."

"That's all they've been getting anyway."

"Where's your spirit?" says R. "Where's your love of free-dom?"

"If there exists a kind of freedom that can be advanced by bad writing, I don't want any part of it. Here's how much I like freedom. I'll take your job and write in my own way: more journals. They can take it or leave it!"

R. is so startled he snaps off the radio, and in the sudden, unusual silence, he shouts in my face:

"WHAT! Then you'd best come with me, because you'll have everybody against you. The Nazis will throw you in Dachau, and tho Americans will be glad to see you go! It's suicide!"

"You really want me to take your place?"

"Yes, I mean what I say."

"I will only do so under those conditions."

R. throws up his hands, and strides to the door and back, and takes a loose cigarette out of his pocket, and sticks it in his mouth, and strikes a match, and turns on the radio again.

"Okay," he says, "suit yourself. It's a waste of time. But I can at least tell them, over there, I left with the under-standing you were going to send what you thought was *news* over. How am I to guess you plan to send out stories in an invented language! Dirty stories at that!"

"I plan to write my journals anyway," I say. "I have a lot more things to talk about. Personally, I believe my journals would make admirable reading over the radio. If I get a chance to do it, why shouldn't I try?"

"They'll never let you near a microphone with this line of yours," says R., turning over the pages of my manuscript. "Here it says the English are as brave as movie stars. Here it says the English love Oxo. Everybody knows the Eng-lish are as brave as movie stars and that they love Oxo, but how do you think the Germans will stomach that? Here it says the English are musical."

"Where do I say the English are musical?"

"That's practically all you talk about: how they sing 'Oh, Johnny, Oh, Johnny.' It's all right to be pro-British, old man: after all, we all are. But you might tone it down a little bit. But what's this: here you say the Germans are musical too, gay, eternally young? Which are you, pro-British or pro-German?"

"Don't let it worry you. As a matter of fact I'm not for any side in any war. I believe in peace. But now I will ask you to do something for me."

The speech on the radio ceases and gives way to the formless, tormented, and somber music of some romantic violins, cellos, and trombones: descriptive music, meant to evoke the sea, lovers, old castles, dark forests, cliffs, birds, clouds, nature, and white, indefinite heroes.

"I can guess what it is you want me to do," says R., "smuggle this journal of yours out of the country."

"Will you take it to America for me, and give it to my agent?"

"You realize what you are asking of me!"

"I swear the censors have nothing against me. They have seen the book, and given it back to me. You aren't risking anything. Will you do it?"

The music swells in the radio. R. frowns with a kind of pride and says:

"Nobody ever said I wasn't the best of sports. You're doing something for me. I'll do something for you. Who's your agent?" He sighs, holding the manuscript under his arm, while I scribble an address on a piece of paper. Then R. completes his statement:

"But I'll only take the thing out of the country for you. I'll take it as far as Lisbon. From there it goes by mail, or freight, or whatever way you choose: I am not going to get nicked for bringing pornography into the United States."

"Here," I say, "here's money for stamps. Send it air mail, from Lisbon," and I fill his hands with money, which he accepts, perplexed, and stuffs into his pocket. His lips prepare to make some further statement, formally urging me to leave, also. His lips prepare his farewells. I will watch the manuscript going downstairs, under his arm. I will watch him, at the bottom of the stairs, hide it under his coat.

The radio talks all the way down the stairs. When he reaches the ground floor, R. puts up my manuscript under his coat, and hides it. He pushes open the hotel door, and assumes a new, rude, important, busy look, and walks out into the street.

I am filled with anguish, at parting with the work I have so dangerously wrought! My book, precious as an only child, goes off on a terrible journey, in the hands of a maniac who believes he understands world affairs, political rights and wrongs, and what is going to happen in the war!

Vada, mi librito, creatura, mis entrañas!

Apartate de mi, corazón!

Yet here is the typewriter and a pile of new paper, white, untouched.

I think suddenly of Blake, filling paper with words, so that the words flew about the room for the angels to read, and after that, what if the paper was lost or destroyed?

That is the only reason for wanting to write, Blake's reason.